Of the same author:
Introduction to Dramatherapy. Person and Threshold
Hove/New York: Brunner/Routledge, 2004

Some praises for *Introduction to Dramatherapy. Person and Threshold:*

"The profoundest book about Dramatherapy that I have read".
Roger Grainger

"I want to read this book again – and again. Thank you, Salvo, for a jewel in the cave".
Sue Jennings

"Salvo Pitruzzella has written a fresh and compelling introductory text on Dramatherapy, embedding his discussion in the solid ground of the social sciences and the contemporary dramatic arts".
Robert Landy, NY University

"It is a book that offers a rich theoretical framework to Dramatherapy".
Kate Kirk, *British Journal of Psychodrama and Sociodrama*

"This book is one of the most important contributions to the dramatherapy canon in recent years. I cannot recommend it too highly".
Anna Seymour, *Dramatherapy Journal*

Salvo Pitruzzella

The Mysterious Guest

An enquiry on creativity from Arts Therapy's perspective.

iUniverse, Inc.
New York   Bloomington

iUniverse books may be ordered through booksellers or by contacting:

iUniverse
1663 Liberty Drive
Bloomington, IN 47403
www.iuniverse.com
1-800-Authors (1-800-288-4677)

ISBN: 978-1-4401-6723-2 (pbk)
ISBN: 978-1-4401-6724-9 (ebk)

Printed in the United States of America

iUniverse rev. date: 8/19/2009

This book is in memory of Roberto Pitruzzella and Giuseppe Leopizzi
"Be glad, for the song has no ending"

Table of Contents

Chapter 17: *Guiding the creative process*

Epilogue: *On being creative in times of destruction*

Introduction

"O brothers, who amid a hundred thousand
Perils", I said, "have come unto the West,
To this so inconsiderable vigil
Which is remaining of your senses still
Be ye unwilling to deny the knowledge,
Following the sun, of the unpeopled world.
Consider ye the seed from which ye sprang;
Ye were not made to live like unto brutes,
But for pursuit of virtue and of knowledge".
(Dante Alighieri, *Inferno, XXVI,* transl. H.W. Longfellow)

"Consider ye the seed from which ye sprang"

Which argument does Ulysses put forward to persuade what remains of his crew to undertake the last journey beyond the Pillars of Hercules, towards the unknown world? Neither the promise of gold and glory, nor the hope of coming back home: only the desire to know, "to be experienced of the world, / And of the vice and virtue of mankind". The mariners are old and weary, they feel the weight of a harsh and seemingly endless war and of a journey that plunged them into a situation wrought with more labours, pain and shame, though it was supposed to bring them back home, to their families and safety. They might have hoped to bring home with them some huge amount of booty, and live the rest of their lives as wealthy, safe, and respected men. All they had had were years and years of distress (some of them spent as pigs); now they are urged again to undertake a last adventure, beyond the beyond, past the world's boundaries, towards unknown wonders and certain perils. We can imagine a look of uncertainty making its way through the wrinkles of their faces, as their brows contract in a doubtful frown. And silence. However, the old captain knows how to manage them: with his "brief exhortation" he appeals to their deepest natures, he advises them to turn inwards, to those qualities that set men apart from beasts, and urges us in pursuit of "virtue and knowledge". Is it perhaps a new ruse of the cunning Ulysses, to be atoned for in fire, along with the evil counsellors, like the other despicable stratagem that ruined the city of Troy? Dante is clearly giving a foretaste of that anxious thirst for discovery that, two centuries later, began turning the world upside down. Nonetheless, being a medieval man, he cannot tolerate such an overt challenge to the limits of humankind, which would be comparable to the sin of Adam. Ulysses' last adventure ends with a sudden tragedy, in which he and his fellows are allowed a brief and blurred vision, which was not destined to become knowledge. In the theocentric universe of Middle Ages, man is merely incidental (woman is even more so), who cannot but conform to the precepts that rule his brief existence. It is not for him to plunge into the unknown, if he does not want to lose his soul.

Personally, I am quite sure that the old hero was, for once, telling the truth. He somehow was agreeing with T.S. Eliot doctrine: "old men ought to be explorers". Accordingly, I accept the main proposition of his argument, "consider ye the seed from which ye sprang". I am inclined to construe it in this way: *the creative principle, which urges us to meet what is new and actively search for it, as we find fulfilment and we enlarge and deepen our humanness in the effort itself, is engraved in our condition as individuals.* It may be hidden beneath strata of fear and uncertainty, oppressed by habitude or by training, frozen when we become objects rather than persons. Yet it remains alive and intact, ready to awaken in the right conditions.

Undoubtedly, such a statement implies an act of faith. There is no experimental evidence that creativity can be considered inherent in human nature, and therefore potentially available to everybody, regardless of any psychic or cultural peculiarity. Carl Gustav Jung describes the creative drive as "a psychic factor whose nature is analogous to the instinct". Unfortunately, when talking about instinct, one ventures onto slippery ground. In one of his enlightening *Metalogues,* Gregory Bateson reminds us that the concept of instinct is "an explanatory tenet, explaining everything you wish to explain with it" (Bateson, 1972: 75). It is quite easy, accordingly, to outline the conditions by which behaviour can be defined as instinctual. Bateson himself, with a grain of irony, lists four of them: "(you can say something is instinctual) when you see a creature doing something and you are sure that: 1, the creature has not learned to do it and, 2, the creature is too silly to understand why she should act like that. 3, when you see that all the members of that species do the same things in the same circumstances; 4, when the animal repeats the same behaviour even when circumstances are changed, and it becomes ineffective" (*ibid*: 82). Moreover, if we try to apply Bateson's conditions to creativity, we may find an impressive chain of ambivalences. 1: is the creative process like an impetus, a spontaneous impulse, or does it rather come out of a lengthy preparation, which includes learning and, sometimes, initiation? 2: is it mostly unaware, or does it bring an intrinsic sense of self-awareness? 3: can everybody be creative, or is it a quality belonging only to few "geniuses" or "talented" persons? 4: is productive achievement (and the resulting acknowledgement by other people) a crucial element for supporting the creative process, or is the process in itself unrelated to any outcome? Strangely enough (but perhaps not too much so), in the extensive field of study and research on creativity, all the hypotheses coexist. We will see it more in detail later.

However, why does Jung need to write about the creative instinct? I am quite sure that it is a matter of experience. Reading his case studies, one is repeatedly surprised by the emergence of artistic forms all through the therapy, which often foreshadow new steps toward healing. And we can imagine that this was an almost constant factor of Jung's work, as he was inspired to devise therapeutic techniques using artistic methods (from the creation of *Mandalas* to "active imagination"). Of course, this is not an explanation at all. It might also be possible that those who went to Jung were the very people who already possessed artistic (and spiritual) receptivity. Alternatively, it seems likely that the personality of the therapist himself acted as a vehicle for indistinct psychical energies, channelling them into artistic solutions. The seed dilemma is still unsolved.

It is true that many people have attempted, guided by different notions of creativity, or even simply following their intuition and sensibility, to introduce into children's education a series of methods and conditions aimed at fostering creative processes, always with good results. It seems that a tolerant environment, and rich in stimuli, an educator able to listen and to support, rather than quick to judge and to punish, and, lastly, the use of techniques devised to set in motion certain qualities of thought, lead to the strengthening of children's natural inclination to discovery, expression and originality. Yet this may seem obvious: it is still hard to understand if it is the awakening of pre-existent potentialities or the by-product of just another educational investment. In other words, human beings are after all quite easy to mould. If I want people to be soldiers, I will set up a strong, authoritarian system of education, and results are guaranteed. In the same way, if I desire a world of original artists, inventors and thinkers, let us develop suitable methods, and many little Michelangelo, Leonardo and Descartes will spring up. Probably a crumb or two of this idea, in a certain way a legacy from Francis Galton, who was patron both of creativity and eugenetic research, lay hidden among the folds of some experimentation, especially in the twenty or so years after 1950, the year when we officially started talking about creativity[1]. These approaches were in connection with a narrow definition of creativity -the only one that can be easily measured- strongly focussed on the cognitive side. It was influenced by the theories of 'divergent thinking' and inclined not to consider other aspects, which are more out of control, like the senses, the emotions and affect. Creativity becomes more and more a 'thinking technology', which can be measured with specific tests. Unsurprisingly, many doubts had arisen on what is measured and how it is, and they have been confirmed in more recent years, calling into question the true value of those tests, and asking for a more qualitative and interactive system of assessment of creativity[2].

We have just begun our journey around creativity, and swarms of questions hinder and confuse us.

Let me try to put some of these questions in order, pivoting around a core issue: what is creativity?

Is it a natural gift or can it be learned?

Is it a common quality or only some special people have it?

Is it something springing from the depths of our innermost self or is it part of our culture?

Can creative products be measured? And processes? And which one is more important?

Many questions and a unique conviction, a sort of faith, impossible to prove: just a little more than some *credo quia absurdum*[3]. "Consider ye the seed from which ye sprang".

When children say Oh

We will linger over all these questions later, not claiming to provide definite and ultimate answers, but in order to paint a picture, vast enough and with enough colours, of the immense world of ideas around this issue. We will try to gather up some concepts that can justify the core hypotheses of this book: creative processes are essential for the healthy development of the individual (as well as groups, communities and societies); their intentional use can be effective in order to redress the balance in those situations where the wholeness of the person is blocked, threatened or compromised.

---

1   1950 is the year of the J.P. Guilford's lecture at APA, which aroused the interest of the psychologists on the topic.
2   See Sternberg & Lubart, 1995; Sternberg (ed.), 1999.
3   Which I like to remember in Alfred Jarry's playful and ambiguous adaptation: "Credo quia absurdum... non credere".

However, since I made a statement of belief, before entering into the argument I would like to tell you something about the journey that brought me to that quiet but firm conviction. I do not want to persuade anybody (or perhaps, since it is a matter of faith, I should say "convert"): I do not have enough poetic tools to construct a "brief exhortation" as synthetic and moving as the words Dante has Ulysses say[4]. It is just a little story told to explain (even to myself) what urged me to write this book.

In the mid-seventies, I was a restless young man, with a thirst for experiences that might give a sense to my search for deep meanings, which I had found neither in religion nor in politics. I joined a circle of young artists, actually rather odd, and eventually, almost unwittingly, I found myself involved first in extemporaneous experiences of street theatre, then in a theatre company for children. We used masks and puppets, shadows and marionettes, music, songs and rhymes, *clowneries* and Chaplin-like gags, and all sorts of hand-made stage machinery (the *capocomico* was a painter, stage designer, and inventor). The step from this experience to working directly with children was quite short. The *spettacol-azione* (play-action) was an immediate way of entering with the children into the shared experience of a great play that could evolve in any way at all. A crocodile steps into the classroom, trying to communicate in an unknown language; a scientist claims to have invented a machine that can take pictures of dreams; a castle is erected with human-size cards, or a house with transparent walls, to be lived in; a bizarre circus comes to look for new attractions. And so on. The children immediately entered that fantasy world (well aware that it was just make-believe), and invented all the possible solutions, in which there was room for both reasonable and absurd ideas. By sculpting, painting, making poems and devising plots, creating masks and puppets, acting, dancing and handling objects as if they were alive, children re-created the world. And the new one was always a world in which the values of encountering, listening, and peace were fundamental.

It's no accident that the movement that in Italy has been called *animazione* (animation) had since the beginning been in contact with other pedagogical experiences, which put children at the very centre of the education process, taking into account their 'culture' (what children already know before going to school), and working constantly in a spirit of respect and research[5]. Over a period of fifteen years, I became acquainted with thousands of children, of all ages and social conditions, from the kindergarten kids of the wealthy city, to the hot-headed adolescents of suburbia. And the amazing fact was that all the time it was enough to open up a space, give trust, and be receptive for the miracle to happen once again. All this was called creativity, a word that was then beginning to become widespread in society, along with a general awareness that something was lacking, something we may have lost while building up a square and predictable world. What it was, there was no need to explain. You could see it in the things themselves: songs, colours, and smiles. If I have learned to believe in creativity that dwells in everyone, I have learned it from the children.

---

4   By the way: comparing in the titles of these paragraphs the words of the divine poet with those of a
     popular pop song is not a disrespectful whim. It just shows how certain attitudes towards the world of
     children are present both in popular culture and in common feeling.
5   I am referring to the seminal experiences of Mario Lodi, inspired in its turn by the "people's pedagogy"
     of Celestin Freinet, and Don Lorenzo Milani's "pedagogic gospel".

The town that was not there

Yet the story has a turning point. In 1989, the group I worked with had the job of running a drama workshop in a psychiatric Therapeutic Community. I tried to gather information that could help us in our work, but found very little. We could only rely on our own resources. Therefore, we had the idea of applying the technique of the "integrating background"[6]: a far-reaching, single narrative that could be used as a framework vast enough to encompass all possible contributions, and clear-cut enough to stand as a guide in the midst of the chaos. The story was an adaptation of a well known Sicilian folk legend (which is a variation of a mythical theme known worldwide[7]). It is called "truvatura" (finding), and it tells of a traveller who, in the night, comes upon a mysterious town (often described as a land of abundance, or concealing a precious treasure), which disappears at dawn, and nobody is then able to find it again. In selecting the story, it was our desire to pass the Pillars of Hercules towards the enigmatic and disturbing world called madness; towards our own fears, too. We asked the patients to help us to invent this town (regardless of whether it existed or not), and to fill it with people, things and events. The results were amazing: we met people who slowly but surely emerged from their everyday dullness, revealing themselves alive and creative, able to approach the game of art with joy and enthusiasm. I cherish the memory of a particular episode. The group had created a sort of dark fairy-tale, with no happy ending: the story of a country ruled by a treacherous tyrant, called King *Manciaracina (Grape-eater,* from the traditional name of a rather nondescript fish), who sent his subjects into exile, even for no reason, in a dark and impenetrable forest, from which they were never to return. We set up the forest (made of paper bands hanging from the ceiling), and improvise the scene. The improvisation begins, lively and inventive: the characters meet, recognise each other, tell their stories, and complain to each other of the cruel fate that has led them there. However, in about fifteen minutes a sensation that something is missing, a sense of stagnation begins to arise, and a strange feeling, swinging from boredom to anxiety begins to work its way within the group. There is no escape route from the forest; it seems that there is nothing to do but stop working and cheer the group up in some other way (like talking, or having a tea). Then a voice is heard, that has never been heard before. It is the voice of an old gentleman, a former in-patient of the old Psychiatric Hospital. We only know his name, Armando, and the fact that before his internment he had worked in his village as a tailor. He speaks quavering, as someone not accustomed to being listened to, but what he says is very clear: at some point of the story, an enormous thunderstorm breaks out in the forest. It seems that the situation is getting even worse, but Armando, unexpectedly, begins to recite a rhyming couplet: "e alluminati du lampu e da saitta/truvaru na gruttuzza stritta stritta"[8]. Little by little, everybody starts to become involved, and the scene takes on a sudden new impetus: we improvise a passage in the cave, which becomes a long and winding tunnel, ending right in the hall of the king. The king (a giant puppet) is beaten and chased away, and in the end everybody is laughing (I would call it cathartic laughter). The event is then celebrated with a long poem, to which everyone gives a contribution.

---

6   See Canevaro, 1988.

7   The episode of Parsifal's finding of Montsalvasche, the Grail castle (in Wolfram von Eschenbach's *Parzival,* as in many other texts of the various Grail traditions) is one of the most well known versions.

8   "And illumed by thunderbolt and lightning/they found a tiny little cave".

However, apart from the enthusiasm, new questions were arising. Was that experience only a pleasant distraction from the humdrum life of the community, or could it really be a help for those waiting souls, a means to recover the previous state of well-being they had lost because of illness, and subsequent alienation (with which the medical structures were often complying)? Therefore, through those sparks of life in persons who seemed extinguished, through those moments of "thawing" – as a psychiatrist friend used to say – we could figure out their inner worlds, fertile and original, that illness had left intact. Were they fated to be opened up only then, in the two hours of this activity, or could they be preserved in some way, as resources for encountering the world outside? In other words: was the creative process (whatever this expression means) a real way towards change, or were we just playing?

I needed to learn more, so I began from theatre itself: the artistic language I loved the best, of all the various ones I had been playing with for all those years (I also had a degree from a well-known drama school). I studied Psychodrama and Dramatherapy (and also other methods of applied theatre, like Jonathan Fox's *Playback Theatre*, Augusto Boal's *Theatre of the Oppressed* and Viola Spolin's *Improvisation*), trying to distil from them some practical cues, concepts and suggestions that could help me to improve my work, and make it more effective. Dramatherapy in particular was the more fascinating for me, because of its positively artistic approach. Moreover, it has its place within the larger framework of Creative Arts Therapies, which includes Art Therapy, Music Therapy and Dance Therapy, connected by the shared idea of using artistic methods for the improvement of people's well-being. New horizons opened up before me: I discovered that I was not alone in searching for a more careful, controlled and conscious application of those processes that I had enthusiastically experimented with in those years of rich and chaotic experiences. In 1998, I joined the Arts Therapies Training Centre in Lecco, Italy, made up of four schools concerned with the main disciplines in the field. My encounters with many colleagues of various school of thoughts and my exchanges of ideas with them, both informally and in conferences, made me understand a little more of the theoretical and practical universes of the other disciplines (though not to the point of applying them myself), and find new questions. Once again, these questions have to do with the meaning of creativity. However, let us proceed in an orderly fashion, and go and have a look at the various ways in which Arts Therapies are applied and conceived, starting from the one I know best, Dramatherapy.

The (arcane) healing virtues of the Arts

Dramatherapy explores the meaningful elements of the dramatic process (actors and their preparation, stage, dramaturgy and direction, dramatic action, audience), holding them both as metaphors to describe the features and the makings of human identity in a world of relationships, and as actual tools for helping people recover from troublesome and painful situations[9]. In the same way, Art Therapy, Music Therapy and Dance Therapy have developed a means of interpreting the aesthetic elements of the languages they use (for example: form, colour and use of material in Art Therapy; rhythm, timbre and sound dynamics in Music Therapy; shape and quality of the movement in Dance Therapy) in order to understand the

---

9   You can find a reasoned synthesis of this in my book *Introduction to Dramatherapy. Person and Threshold*, Hove/New York: Brunner/Routledge, 2004.

client's world. At the same time, they apply them in order to stimulate the motions toward transformation in the clients themselves.

In spite of the variety of styles and approaches that characterise the manifold archipelago of Creative Arts Therapies, we can also identify some important methodological similarities, mainly those that concern the use of specific structures of the artistic process, which we may define by the following terms: *training*; *improvisation*; *composition*.

Training is the first contact with the specific features of the various artistic languages. It is not aimed at learning already established codes or the "right" communication techniques, but rather at encouraging people to experience the languages themselves, looking for their own particular expression. In groups, it is often presented in the form of a series of games and exercises, helping to work at the same time on interpersonal relationships and collaboration.

Improvisations are the free and immediate applications of the languages explored. They can be individual or group improvisations; they can be totally free or partly planned (for example: they may or may not have a planned topic or plot). They are the space in which people reveal themselves, through the mediating metaphor of the expressive language, and actively search for new patterns and new meanings through interaction with the others and with the therapist.

Compositions are the deliberate expressive plans, made by individuals or groups. They include gathering ideas, refining them, and actively looking for the way to express them properly. In these compositions, spontaneity is interwoven with knowledge, and the need to communicate plays a key role.

Another common feature in almost all the approaches of the Arts Therapies is the need for of some way of *reworking* the experience, achieved by the group or by the individual with the help of the therapist. Such reworking can be done with words, or through ritualised activities, using symbolic communication. It can be restricted to a sharing of the feelings, or developed in a detailed analysis of the experience. Therefore, the kind of presence required from the therapist can be very different in each approach: a range of actions going from facilitating interpersonal exchange to suggesting hidden meanings.

There are, then, both important analogies and meaningful differences in the methodological approaches of the Arts Therapies, underscored by the various ways of looking at the role of therapist, outlined above. Let me emphasise the fact that these differences can be seen within the bounds of each separate discipline, portraying a variety of styles, sometimes compatible or quite complementary, sometimes so distant from each other. This means that a single theoretical paradigm of the Arts Therapies is far from existing, and, what is more, within each discipline different paradigms coexist, which only partially overlap. And I believe that this area of overlapping, this common denominator, can be found in creativity.

Let us try to identify two tendencies, which mark the main differences in style.

In the first, the understanding of the person and his/her issues is connected to the theoretical foundations of the psychotherapies, mainly in the psychodynamic area. In this approach, the verbal reworking of the experience, often in the form of an interpretation by the therapist, has a central role, and the artistic process tends to become a mere instrument for eliciting meanings that will then be better understood through words. With regard to the issue of creativity, sometimes there is a little embarrassment, since the classical psychoanalysts, and most of their followers (with some important exceptions, like the already quoted Winnicott, of whom we will discuss later), did not take creativity very much into consideration, or they related it, directly or indirectly, to pathological states.

The second is more eclectic, embracing concepts both from the area of psychology and from other disciplines within the humanities. It founds its conception of the therapeutic process on its intrinsic artistic quality, that encourages a new attitude towards the world and, eventually, a new vision of oneself. The risk here is that a tautological idea of creativity may be developed, identifying it *tout court* with the artistic process –which, by its very nature, includes some obscure and indefinable aspects- and forgoes a thorough examination of the connections between the creative process and well-being.

Actually, we must consider these tendencies as extreme examples, as they are seldom found in the way described above. In between, there is an abundance of approaches through which the two tendencies are intermingled, and often enriched, with contributions from other fields. But whatever the theoretical and methodological attitude may be, it is also beyond doubt that all the approaches give a particular value to creativity. And they do so largely out of experience: the vast majority of Arts Therapies practitioners have direct acquaintance with the artistic language they use; many are putting them into practice all the time, professionally, or as amateurs.

My impression is that a coherent concept of what creativity is and its connections with the person's well-being, is implicit at the roots of the practice of Arts Therapies. It is difficult to explore it at a theoretical level because to be involved in a creative process is not the same as observing it at a distance, perhaps by reading about it. Day by day, those who apply Arts Therapies live through the creative processes that flow out from within their groups, as well as their own. Creative experiences contain an element of mystery, which reminds us of what Isadora Duncan used to say: "If I could say it with words, there would be no need to dance it"; something we fear might be spoilt if revealed.

I believe that it is possible and necessary to undertake this exploration, with grace and gentleness in order to avoid ruining the enchantment of the mystery. The book you are reading is intended to be an initial contribution with this aim in view. It is addressed to all Arts Therapies practitioners and students, as well as to professionals and students in the fields of healthcare, education, and social welfare, who are interested in creativity. I hope it can also be used by anyone who aims at cultivating his or her own personal creativity.

Between vision and reason: the journey within this book

Until now, I have been telling you of the long incubatory path of this book. However, there is also a pathway within the book itself that I will try to outline as a map for the reader.

The First part, *In search of creativity*, is a short guided tour into the immense land of ideas on the subject, in order to understand the answers that have been supplied to the questions that we asked previously, the most important of which is: what is creativity, and where does it come from? Such a tour may seem neither objective nor comprehensive: many are the points of view, and sometimes the most interesting are so unsuitable as to appear even in conflict with each other. It is a vain effort to try to compare the various concepts of creativity in order to extract a single framework. Therefore, I have to admit certain arbitrariness in my choices, favouring those points of view that not only see creativity as a potential quality possessed by all the individuals, but also as an essential element of the personality, as important as affect and cognition, which, just like these, needs to be cultivated, educated and, sometimes, treated.

In the Second part, *Creativity as a Feature of Being a Person*, I start from the hypothesis previously stated (that creativity is an essential element of human personality), trying to discuss the benefits that healthy creativity may bring to the person's psychic balance. So I synthesised the features in which creativity is expressed in person's life, namely: those ways of encountering the world that are already present in children, which can be awakened and adjusted in adult life, in order to become new opportunities for the transformation of those conditions that block the full realization of our potentialities.[10] From such an assumption, I tried to develop the hypothesis, which I consider the core of the Arts Therapies: that direct experimentation with the creative processes can be a contribution to this awakening.

We now have some ideas of what creativity is and why it is useful, but still we do not know *how* it works. It is necessary to go deeper into the heart of the creative process.

The Third part, *The roots of creativity*, explores some aspects of the most popular theories of the creative process, deriving from them a hypothesis about how the process itself works.

Such hypothesis is deepened in the Fourth part, *Elements of the creative process*, displaying a model of the creative process as the dynamic interplay of four main factors, on whose interactions both the equilibrium of the process itself, and its potentiality to improve a person's well-being depend. This model is the fruit of years of study and first hand observation of creative processes in all kinds of groups and situations. Above all, what inspired me is the "fourfold vision" of the poet William Blake.

The model is further investigated with a detailed analysis of what I have identified as the four main factors (Imagination, Spontaneity, Self-listening and Productiveness) and of the different ways in which they interact.[11] A thorough inquiry into these combinations can be, in my opinion, an effective tool to comprehend both individual and group creativity, and to offer methods for directing the creative processes towards developmental outcomes, in any of the fields in which they may be used (education, therapy and rehabilitation, adult training, community policies and applied arts).

A chapter then follows dealing with the attitude of the therapist, who must keep a constant balance between his own creative insights and his control of the situation (once again: vision and reason), in order to avoid one aspect overwhelming the other. Here, too, the fourfold model previously presented can provide useful suggestions for everyday work.

It will be often a journey through winding roads, where we will have many meetings, and many stories to tell. More than once, the stages will be points of departure for further short journeys in contiguous territories, to deepen the roots of this or that concept. Eventually, we will probably have some answer to the many questions we outlined in this introduction, and, I hope, a few more questions.

If the itinerary proposed meets your approval, then let us get ready to go.

---

10 Part of this synthesis has already been treated in a lecture at the IV Yearly Conference of the Arts Therapies Training Centre of Lecco (May 2005).

11 A first version of the model can be found in the introduction of my book *Manuale di Teatro Creativo*, Milano: Franco Angeli, 2004.

First Part

In search of creativity

"Tyger Tyger, burning bright,
In the forests of the night;
What immortal hand or eye,
Could frame thy fearful symmetry?
(...)
When the stars threw down their spears
And water'd heavens with their tears:
Did he smile his work to see?
Did the one who made the Lamb make thee?"
(William Blake, *The Tyger*)

"A composer is a guy who goes around forcing his will on
unsuspecting air molecules".
(Frank Zappa)

1. Creation.

Gods and humans

"Nobody knows where water came from. Nobody knows where Old Man Coyote came from. Yet he existed, he lived. So spoke Old Man Coyote: 'It's not good that I am here all alone. I need someone to talk to. It's not good that there is only water and nothing else'. Old Man Coyote walked around, and he spied someone living: two red-eyed ducks" (Erdoes, Ortiz, 1989: 146).

The ancient Crow legend goes that the Old Man Coyote, who had provisionally quitted his role as a trickster, and acts as a world creator, sends his new companions on an underwater expedition, to find out if there is a bottom. After many attempts, one of the ducks brings up a tiny root.

"Good heavens, it's a root!" he said, "and where roots are, there must be some soil. My younger brothers, please dive once more. If you find something soft, bring it out". So the duck went down for the third time, and he emerged with a soft clod of earth in his beak. Old Man Coyote examined it. "Ah, my younger brothers, this is just what I wanted. I'll make it big. I'll spread it all around. This little handful of mud will be our dwelling". Old Man Coyote blew upon the clod, and it grew bigger and bigger, and started spreading everywhere. "What a surprise, older brother, the ducks said. It's wonderful. We are delighted" (ibid: 147). Then Old Man Coyote sticks the root in the mud, and the whole creation of the world starts to begin.

Narratives like this are usually found in many traditional cultures. In them, the characters creating the world confer shape and function to some undifferentiated pre-existent substance: they do not engender it from themselves, nor produce it from nothing through an intentional deed. Our Christian tradition emphasizes instead this latter aspect, the creation *ex nihilo*, because conceiving something that exists outside God himself would be a diminution of his qualities. Thus, the only genuine creative power is God's: human beings may imitate, reproduce, or rearrange, but they cannot properly create. It is commonly held that this idea is in the Bible, but this is not actually true. In *Genesis* (I, 1) it is indeed written that God created heaven and earth, but there is no hint about a creation coming from nothing. On the contrary, in the *Book of Wisdom* (XI, 17) the earth is created from "an invisible matter". Insisting on creation *ex nihilo* derives from the bitter polemics that the Fathers of the Church raised against the Gnostic sects flourishing in the first centuries of Christian Age.

The Gnostics had recovered from Plato the notion of a demiurge, a sort of low-level creator, who is responsible for the imperfection of the material world. It was quite an ambivalent claim: on the one hand, it could have solved drastically the question of the origins of evil; on the other hand, it introduced a dangerous dualistic stance, which demanded to be harshly thwarted. It would reappear, some centuries later, in the Cathar heresy, repressed with bloodshed. Gnostics had built a complex theological system, somewhat obscure and contradictory, which has only been studied recently. Let me briefly express a couple of impressions about it (not claiming to be historically or scientifically correct). First: the supreme God does not create, but emanates from himself other spiritual entities (as in Plotinus and the Neoplatonists). The last emanation is the demiurge, who creates the world turning spirit into matter. Matter is therefore fallen spirit, and it has a negative value: the material world, including our very body, is despicable. This point of view on body and matter, although not entirely coherent with Christian ideas, is however not so outrageous: let us remember the attitude of the Catholic Church towards sex. In this way, the Gnostics were not revolutionary at all.

Spheres

Yet another interesting aspect is that, all in all, there is some affinity between the Gnostic demiurge and our Old Man Coyote.

It is written in the *Origins of the world,* a Gnostic text found among the Nag-Hammadi manuscripts: "When the demiurge noticed his own greatness – he saw only himself and nothing else but darkness and water – he thought he was the only existing thing. His thought was accomplished with his word. He manifested himself as a wind hovering upon the waters. Then he divided the watery substance on one side and the dry substance on the other side; with one of the substances, he made himself a dwelling, and he called it 'heaven', with the other, he made himself a stool, and he called it 'earth'" (Moraldi, 1982: 219).

In the immense mythological corpus of the Native Americans, Old Man Coyote is the character who, more than any other, embodies the figure of the *trickster,* the "divine fool". Cunning and a blunderer, clumsy and wise, sometimes egoistic and wicked, sometimes playful and cheeky, the *trickster* constantly challenges the order of the world. As a demiurge, he is liable for the world's flaws, often a consequence of some unsuccessful experiment. However, these flaws are exactly what preserves the world from immobility and sets history in motion.

Christian orthodoxy could not accept the notion of matter pre-existing the creator himself, nor the image of a maladroit creation made through experiments and of a creator acting by "trial and error". This denial would be, in the Modern Age, one of the causes of the relentless conflict between science and faith.

The more the physical world was questioned, from celestial bodies to living organisms, and the laws regulating their actions were stated, the harder it became to uphold the idea of a God as a unique ruler of the world. Unless used as a metaphor: from Galileo up to the followers of Enlightenment, very few scientists and philosophers claimed to be atheists. They ended up, however, banishing God on the fringe of creation, as a principle setting up the process and establishing its laws, but eventually not so much interested in the fate of the created world, or in human events.[12] William Blake, who lived in the earth of Enlightenment age, had prophetically warned against such a tendency, which he generally called "deism". On the one hand, it relieved us from the burden of a religion controlling every depth of our lives; on the

---

12   Yet the hardest blow to the traditional conceptions of a divine creation was from the archaeological researches and the theory of evolution. The former forced us to backdate the chronology of the world's history, so questioning the letter itself of the biblical narrative. The second, contrasting the account of man's creation, replaced the divine intervention with natural laws.

other hand, entrusting the understanding of the world to sheer reason, and cleaning it ever more from any spiritual principle, it ended in denying the creative nature of human beings. The meticulous likelihood pursued by the painters of his age, who, according to Blake "mock Inspiration and Vision", is a case in point. For Blake, creation is unceasingly renewing itself, and human beings participate in it through their deepest human quality, the "Poetic Genius". Art therefore is not imitating reality but revealing it through the act of re-creating it.

Yet let us go back to our story. After creating the world, with plants, trees, lakes and mountains, Old Man Coyote talks again to the ducks. "Well, my younger brothers, is there anything I forgot? What do your hearts say?' 'Older brother, everything is fine. What could be missed?' 'We need some companions. We are so lonely. It is boring'. Thus, he took a handful of mud, and made people from it. How he did so, no one can even imagine".

Can we imagine it? "Then the Lord moulded man with the dust of the soil, and blew into his nostrils a breath of life, and man became a living being" (*Genesis*, II, 7).

These narratives conjure up two powerful, conflicting images.

The first shows the creation from nothing: "What was not before, is now" (Anselmo d'Aosta, *Monologion*, 8). This is the guiding image of the sphere of *novelty*.

The second shows the rearrangement of pre-existent realities. This is the guiding image of the sphere of *transformation*.

This little foray in the realms of myth helps us to reflect on the different nuances of the meaning of the word "creation". If we move back to the ground of human experience, the two images are far from being inconsistent, but rather complementary, and they describe two key aspects of creativity. Let us explore them further.

2. Novelty

The concept of novelty has to do with difference. What can we define as new?

We may think about time flowing. We may say: today is another day. There is in Sicily an ancient idiom saying: "night or day, it's always a day", echoing an archaic feeling of resignation. Every day is like another, predictable and recurring. But if we say: today is a new day, we voice hope and curiosity, the chance that today might be different from yesterday. Something is new when it is different from the members of its class preceding it. Obviously enough, the threshold of significance is subjective: I perceive the difference according to my experience.

Originality

On the subject of human creativity, the criterion has been defined in terms of *originality*. Any product (an object, an idea, an action, even a feeling) is original when the elements of novelty within it are able to produce a *qualitative leap*, implying its ascription to a different order.

To understand it better, we may consider how the history of sciences has always been punctuated with these kinds of leaps. According to Thomas Kuhn's renowned model, there are times when science spins around itself, and scientists become nothing more than puzzle-solvers within a framework that is basically dormant. Such a situation endures until the intervention of a single scientist, or of a group of them, revolutionizes the paradigm of reference (the system of theories, values, and proceedings shared by a scientific community and based on former discoveries, and also the terminology expressing it). Such a revolution produces a discontinuity generating new paradigms and the possibility of new discoveries. The history of arts follows a comparable pattern. Often the action of an artist or of an artistic group disrupts an established routine, challenging the very notion of art. This phenomenon was especially evident in the last Century, when cultural sea-changes and their subsequent circulation happened at a striking speed. If Impressionism and Expressionism had already shaken the idea of perception, in Abstractionism the concept itself of representing is revised. Similarly, Wagner and Mahler had forced the constraints of tonality, but it is with Schoenberg and Stravinsky that they collapse. At times, the innovators are voices in the desert, whose originality is neither acknowledged nor appreciated by their contemporaries, yet it returns later in time, influencing powerfully the upcoming artistic phenomena. Antonin Artaud is a case in point: he died poor and mad, but his heritage, many years later, triggered an earthquake upsetting the whole theatrical scenario in the post-war period, forcing theatre to put itself in question. From the point of view of the novelty maker, the possibility of originality connects with courage: the more the norms that rule paradigms are powerful, the more courage is needed to break them. Mozart had risked his career many times, making operas that defied tradition, and inserting "devilish" intervals in his quartets: if he had lived in the Nazi age, that banned "degenerate" art, he would probably have risked his life. The great humanistic psychologist Rollo May elects as a patron of the artist the Myth of Prometheus, because in the creative act "an active battle with the gods is occurring" (May, 1975: 27). On the opposite side of the psychological universe, Robert J. Sternberg, one of the pioneers of creativity research from a cognitive standpoint, maintains that "the pressure for conformity is usually strong, and the possibility to make a colossal fool of oneself by disagreeing with the crowd always lurks. Yet, to be creative, one needs to take that risk" (Sternberg & Lubart, 1995: 8). Two centuries earlier, William Blake wrote, "I must Create a System, or be enslav'd by another Mans" (*Jerusalem*, 10:20).

Surprise

Originality manifests itself through *surprise*, both in the creator and in the observer. Surprise is sometimes accompanied by uncomfortable feelings, when a creative product is so far from expectations to become disturbing. This often engenders negative reactions: theatre history is filled with "scandalous premieres", from Pirandello's *Six characters in search of an author* to Living Theatre's *Paradise Now!* Jerome Bruner writes of "productive surprise", "the unexpected that strikes the observer with astonishment and wonder" (Bruner, 1964: 43). He continues underscoring the fact that often, after the first amazement, what is new becomes obvious: discoveries that seemed revolutionary in the beginning are now absolutely normal. Bruner takes Einstein's relativity theory as an example, but countless occurrences in art and science can confirm it: from the Copernican system to the fragmentation of the human figure accomplished by Pablo Picasso. According to Erich Fromm, "the premise of any creation, either in science or in art" is "the ability to feel perplexed" (Fromm, 1959: 72). His idea is that this ability is intrinsic to children's experience of the world. "All their hard labour consists in the attempt to find their way in a new world, to grab the meaning of constant new things they learn through experience. They are perplexed, surprised, able to wonder...yet the majority of people lose this ability to admire and be amazed, once introduced to the education processes" (*ibid*).

We can refer this discussion to the tension between *assimilation* and *accommodation*, devised by Jean Piaget to describe the learning processes. Our relationship with the world is not a definitive and unquestionable datum, but a dynamic process, constantly developing new synthesis, made of associations, categories, and hierarchies: making connections between the elements of the reality we live is an attempt to find an order in the perceptive chaos surrounding us. Children meeting the world do nothing but build it within themselves like bricks of a construction toy: each piece joins the others, producing distinct shapes, both provisional and steady, giving experience a sense, and allowing us to anticipate events. When a new event appears within our horizon, and we decide not to ignore it, we have two options: we can try to understand it by assimilating it into our schemes, or modify such schemes in order to receive it. In both cases, we face risk. In the first case, the risk is to grasp just a tiny bit of the event, little enough to leave our schemes safe and sound, so missing the developmental chance it offers. In the second case, the risk it that our toy building falls down and shatters, leaving us in chaos and unable to judge. A stable balance between these polarities is hard to conceive. We can only say that a construction near to equilibrium should be at the same time flexible enough and complex enough. The fact is that only a portion (probably rather scarce) of the schemes that shape experience and give meaning to it is subdued to an examination by our consciousness. The rest is a shadowy place, made of fragments of moments, ancient drives, images and, sometimes, hindrances and violence, which our conscious selves ignore; a place seldom explored in everyday life. Factors that are mysterious even for us come into play in our relationship with novelty. Often, the domains merge, and we lay claim to take decision with our reason where feelings should govern, and vice versa. Maybe the maddened audience of *Six characters* was trying to exorcise the ghost of an upcoming, pandemic identity crisis, which was going to deliver them soon into the hands of merciless tyrants.

In short: facing novelty is a complex and delicate process, only partly governed by consciousness. It involves a movement, a ferment that is, sometimes, a necessary crossing of chaos, whether we meet novelty in our way, or if we are the makers of it. It is however an indispensable process to preserve the world from immobility and sterility.

How is novelty bred into human experience? We will start to reflect upon this point exploring the other pole of our metaphor.

3. Transformation

The visible and the invisible

The verb "to transform" derives from the Latin *transformare*, composed of the prefix *trans*, meaning *beyond, through* and *farther on*, and the verb *formare*. This latter word covers a rather wide range of meanings, related to the complexity of the concept of form.

Giving form to something may involve using hands or tools, words, thoughts or imagination. Body and mind. It is a necessity, because what is formless has no place in our experience of the world: every object (including ourselves) must have a shape to be conceivable. The Western philosophical tradition has insisted on this subject for two thousand years and more. Plato was looking for ideal forms eternally present on a higher level of being (the spiritual world), to which the forms of the world strive to resemble. Aristotle saw the form as an organizing principle, ingrained in matter itself. These two ideas seem to be antithetical, but they are rather complementary if we compare them with Democritus' tenet, searching for the key of appraising reality in the gathering of atoms. Actually, as is noted by L.L.Whyte, from then until now, there has been "a hard struggle between two tendencies of thought: atomism – material analysis – quantitative precision, and form – unity – symmetry" (White, 1968: 31). Form presents itself as a unifying criterion for knowledge, through which the elements of the world get an identity and can be met: this is roughly Kant's opinion.

In our subjective experience, form manifests itself both as *aspect* and as *organization*. The first term refers to the perception of *appearance*: the sensory data tell us about the object we come across, allowing us to discriminate it from the others. The second refers to the comprehension of the *structure*: how its components fit and operate together.

I look at my hand: I can see the outline describing the palm and each of the single five fingers, its pinkish colour, and the lines crossing it. But if I put my attention to the space between the fingers, and to the motions crossing this space, I can perceive the relationships among the hand's elements, which make this hand a human hand.

It is worth noticing that the former of these ways of meeting the form is liable to deception: we may mistake a western movie set for a deserted town. In the stories of Giufà, the wise and foolish character of the Mediterranean tradition, the protagonist picks up a frozen stiff snake thinking it is a stick, or tries to sell a piece of material to a statue. Nonetheless, as we are symbolic animals, we are also able to do the opposite: using a blanket to replace mummy (even if it only stands for a few functions), or worshipping a statue as a god. Gods themselves give us a rather odd example, when human beings under their power turn into trees, springs, animals, yet still keeping their identity. On the other hand, structures not always are perceivable at a first glance: if I were to observe a hand for the first time, and it was motionless, I would probably understand eventually its way of working, but it would take time. Often, the internal organization of an object remains mysterious for a long time.

Meeting a form is both perception and understanding.

Therefore, transforming something means changing aspect and organization, appearance and structure, the visible and the invisible.

I can take the tessera of the *Tangram* game, and rearrange them until I get another figure; I can take milk, eggs, flour, and apples and transform them into a pie; I can take a person… here our analogy starts wearing thin. I heard a wise man uttering that there are three major mistakes in human life: as youngsters, we want to change the world; as adults, we want to change our partners; as elders, we want to change the youngsters. Passing to a more tragic note, the history of mankind is full of countless illustration of how power attempts to transform citizens in something else: soldiers, or even worse. Many of those attempts have yielded disasters.

However, if we consider the domain of the care of psychic diseases, we will see that the issue of transformation is unavoidable. Discarding visible symptoms is not enough to overcome a condition of psychic suffering: it is necessary that people search for a new balance. This research may be advised and accompanied, but never imposed. (This makes psychotherapy such a delicate matter: who is transforming whom?).

Rearrangement

So the topic of psychic care evokes an important meaning of the word transformation, underlining the fact that healing comes from an internal rearrangement. On the terms of such a rearrangement, we will see more when we reflect on the value of creativity in therapeutic processes.

What the above topic suggests is that a real transformation is not limited to a change in external aspect (or in the behaviour, as in the above example), but it must be associated with a significant rearrangement of the internal organization of what is to be transformed. Here we must abandon our example, because a definition of the meaning of people's internal rearrangement would imply a long survey of the theories sustaining the various forms of psycho-therapy (including Arts Therapies). What are indeed psychological theories if not attempts to describe people's internal form?

It would be better to go, for now, to a more trivial example. We could think about bricolage. I find an old battered chest in a junk-dealer shop; I repaint it in sparkling ivory white, and decorate it with flowers. Or else: I find some sea-polished wood and an out-of-fashion straw hat, and I make a reading lamp. Which is the difference between these two transformations? The first retains both the structure and the function of the object, intervening only on its appearance; the second, joining different objects in a single whole, creates a synthesis between elements belonging to distinct areas of experience, ascribing them a different role from to the one they had in their former context. Although it is a case of common creativity, the example prompts new questions on some of the many untied knots about creativity: the relationships between project and intuition, and between process and product, which had often been considered as conflicting. We will try later to demonstrate how in our model of creative process they actually coexist. For the moment, it is better to cling to the effects rather than to the intentions: the chest maintains its own structure, while the wood and the hat are recombined in a new structure.

Regeneration

Both the transformations in our last example, however, share a quality: through them, objects take on a new life. What do we mean by a new life? Here the issue moves from form to history (from space to time), and touches the issue of identity. In order to affirm that an element of the world is nameable in the same way, we must bestow it with an identity, even if it is subjected to incessant changes, which are the essence of time itself. We perceive every object as distinct from another. Although each thing is in relation with many others (according to the mystics everything is related to everything), this can happen because they are separate. The fact that we perceive ourselves as identities (and we cannot do otherwise) has always been a hard nut to crack for psychology since its origin. It is clear that human life is punctuated with so many moments in which the answer to the question "who am I?" is crucial; yet this answer is different each time, and sometimes there is no answer at all. Regeneration, from the subject's standpoint, involves an identity shift, which sometimes means a complete redefinition of it, legitimated by other people's perception. The action of regenerating is strictly tied to the context. In broad terms, any human act is a regeneration act, as it always operates upon pre-existing material: even the most revolutionary innovations in art and science needed something to refute. And if it is true, as we said before, that art and science advance by leaps rather than by accumulation, it is also true that every revolution must have at least a status quo to subvert.

In brief, a first general definition of creativity, wide enough to be useful to describe both high creativity (as science or arts) and everyday creativity, might be the following:

The process that leads, through the regeneration and the rearrangement of pre-existing elements, to the production of something new and original, which engenders surprise both in the creator and in the observer.

Second Part

Creativity as a feature of being a person

"Because we are capable of reflecting upon ourselves,
we are committed, willy-nilly,
to an artistic enterprise in the creation of our own personality"
(Frank Barron)

"Freedom just around the corner for you
But with the truth so far off, what good will it do?
Jokerman dance to the nightingale tune
Bird fly high by the light of the moon
Oh, oh, oh, Jokerman"
(Bob Dylan, *Jokerman*)

4. The creative attitude

A Hocpotus head

It is a warm morning in April, and there is a little crowd of three-year old children laughing and scuffling around me, while I put down a heavy bag full of greenish, damp stuff. "What have you got there?" "Clay" "What is it for?" "For play". "How do you play with clay?" "I'll show you", I say, opening the bag and taking out a small shapeless mound, and then I start squashing and handling it before them. The children gaze charmed, uncertain between distaste and curiosity. Then the latter prevails, and one shyly starts to finger the clay on the bench. Someone else glances questioningly at the teacher, realizing that they may dirty their hands, playing with that thing. As she nods assent, many accept the pieces I offer them, and find a spot in the room to play quietly with their piece of clay. I have given neither instructions nor examples (only showing them it is soft and pliable), so children are free to experiment at their will. There is one who squashes and squeezes it again and again, to hear the sound it makes and one who tastes it and one who smells it. Some bang it on the wall and some flatten it hammering it with their fist. There are some pushing it into holes and some flinging it in the air; and even sticking it on their clothes or in their mates' hair. A big bedlam, through which I notice the worried gaze of the teacher, barely comforted by the fact that, as the day is mild, two big basins of water are ready in the garden.

After various experiments, in which she saw the piece of clay stretching and compacting under her hands, Marina finds a half-egg-shaped plastic container, and she carefully fills it with clay. When it is well stuffed, she tries to extract the content, which comes out smoothly. She takes it in her hands and examines it very carefully, turning it round to observe it from all the perspectives. Then she stops a little while, gripped. All of a sudden, her face brightens, and she whispers, as if talking to herself: "Hocpotus head". Then she raises her head, realizes I was watching her, and smiles at me, uttering: "Look: it's a hocpotus head!" Finally, she starts running with raised arms, keeping her artefact as if it was a torch, laughing and shouting: "Hocpotus! Hocpotus!" The other children crowd around her curiously, while Marina lays the precious little head on a bench and tries to rough out some tiny tentacles. And here the group play begins. First, they put it on a plate, and cut it in slices with a plastic knife: probably, many of them had the chance to see, on a seaside road, the boiled octopuses making a fine show on the sea-food stalls. Then someone remembers that "hocpotuses" live in the sea, and someone else finds a little piece of clay vaguely almond-shaped and provides it with tail, making out a fish. Soon the others follow them, creating quickly a vast undersea environment, with fish families, rocks, seaweed, starfishes, and a rather huge amount of hocpotuses. Many of them look indeed rather odd, but what's the problem if they are so funny? The point is that they are good to play with.

This happened many years ago (Marina is now twenty and studies at the Fine Arts Academy). If I tell it here, it is because it seems convenient enough to help my reflection on creativity. Reflections that will go on considering a set of psychic attitudes and qualities that are crucial conditions for creative processes to grow. My hypothesis is that, while they are in charge of the creative process, the experience of the process itself empowers them, making them stable traits of our personalities. Through them, our balance as individuals is fostered, as well as our ability to aim toward our whole accomplishment, yet facing life's unavoidable changes and challenges.

Obviously, this is an event of "small" creativity, which is not going to influence History like the inventions of the compass, of quantum mechanics or of rock music. However, we can apply our definition of creativity equally to either kind, and what I would like to stress is the fact that the experience of children discovering the world is full of such events. Undoubtedly, children must benefit by a minimum of basic life conditions for their natural inclination towards creativity to be expressed and fulfilled. First, their physiological needs have to be satisfied: if they suffer from hunger or cold, it is quite unlikely that they might be in the best mood. Secondly, they must be provided with enough space to move and time to experiment. Most of all, they must feel safe: under a threat, whether real or fancied, children may find it difficult to concentrate. Safety must be also at an affective level: they must feel loved, accepted, and respected.

The Declaration of Children's Rights proclaimed by UN in 1959 should warrant the fulfilment of these needs, which roughly match the first four levels of the hierarchy of fundamental needs formulated by Abraham Maslow (1954). Does it mean, one would ask, that if the principles of that Declaration were to be respected, all the children in the world would be creative? My answer is yes. To be creative is their job: to discover the world and give it a meaning is an exceedingly creative venture. This does not mean that the condition for creativity is a total and unceasing happiness (nor that mollycoddled children are more creative). Children are continuously exposed to life's crudeness. My Marina, for instance, had lost her father when she was a toddler, but her mother had been able to find the right ways to be close to her, and let her counterbalance the loss. The school's ambience, moreover, was cosy and rich in stimulations; the relationship with the teacher balanced and relaxed.

The emblems of a creative attitude

When these minimal conditions are respected, children are naturally creative. Which are the signs through which this creative inclination manifests itself? I will try to find the main ones taking again into consideration the above episode.

I have said that, after an initial wariness, *curiosity* gets the upper hand: children choose not to ignore novelty, but begin showing interest. Interest is a curious double-faced word: I am interested in something, or something interests me. It is an interesting relationship subject-object: object presents itself as a call to be known, but my intentional turning toward it allows the act of knowledge. To be curious involves a temporary going out of ourselves to meet the object of our curiosity. Marina is no more Marina, but Marina + clay.

This may become especially difficult when the object in question cannot be easily put into our categories of knowledge. Hence, we must be able to welcome all possibilities, even the oddest and the most bewildering, suggested by the relationship with the object. I call this attitude *versatility*. Clay resembles many things: to the touch, it is a bit like mud (and many handle it to feel the effect on their skin), it is easy to manipulate like dough (and many make pizzas), but it can be many more things, and they all need to be experimented with.

Being potentially many things, it risks being nothing at all. This can be hard to tolerate, but children have an ability that is denied to us adults, the ability to plunge entirely into the experience. In child play, we find a quality of engrossment comparable to that of a Yoga master. This allows Marina to be absorbed in experimentation (which gives a pleasure in itself, besides purposes) until the final discovery. This is the quality of *presence*.

These three signs are **the emblems of creative attitude: *Curiosity, Versatility,* and *Presence*.** Curiosity is willingness to encounter; Versatility is willingness to change; Presence is willingness to be. They are all dimensions of experience and personal qualities. They are therefore to be considered as requirement for creative process to take place and at the same times principles founding the creative personality. The latter aspect will be clearer if we go on considering the ways in which they become psychic traits and their developmental function in the making of the person.

5. Curiosity

Our tradition is full of stories warning against curiosity, nearly always portrayed in women. Pandora opens the box where the world's evils are kept locked, and Psyche lights up her husband's countenance, causing him to flee. In *Bluebeard*, which is, according to Italo Calvino, "the prototype of all horror stories", the maiden who opens the forbidden door uncovers her husband's dreadful crimes, risking her life. Charles Perrault, the first to write it down, sketches concise morals: "Curiosity always begets/deep sorrows and regrets./ It's a vain joy (fair sex, you will discover)/that, once reached, soon is over" (Perrault, 1957:12). Why is curiosity so discouraged? First, it has a transgressive quality, as it drives us to infringe rules and prohibitions, and women are not supposed to know as much as men, because this might threaten men's power. Furthermore, Perrault would add, it is an ephemeral pleasure, which dies out as it is satisfied, and leads no further.

Today, of course, the attribution of a negative value to curiosity is not so emphasized. If we look at the way ethology has recounted it, in terms of exploration instinct, we will see it as an attitude playing a crucial role in evolution. Would we have ever discovered fire, without it? Experimental psychology, as Gregory Bateson tells us, demonstrates that it is impossible to "teach a rat not to explore by giving him an electric shock when he pokes his nose in boxes" (1979: 188): all the rat will learn is not to poke his nose in those boxes that, when examined, had given him an electric shock (ibid: 168). With the due reservations about the concept of "instinct" (discussed in the Introduction), curiosity beyond doubt connotes us both as animals and as humans, and it can scarcely be defeated by the moral of any tale.

However, let me linger a little more upon the relation between womanhood and curiosity. The Latin word *cura* stands at the very roots of curiosity. *Cura* means care (rather than cure), and also kindness and concern. This may make us think that curiosity is a way of meeting other people and things, which includes the act of taking care. We can find a poetic synthesis of this in the well known F.E.Burnett's novel *The secret garden*. The little girl Mary, portrayed by the author as a loner, naughty and selfish, will go through a transformation that will take her to discover the importance of human relationship, and to grow in self-awareness. At the beginning of the story, Mary explores the large, bleak mansion where she is a guest, driven mostly by boredom. As soon as she notices that there is a hidden part of the garden, beside a big wall with no door in it, an unknown world inviting her to unveil it, then something begins to change. The encounter with the secret garden coincides with the encounter with her cousin Colin, who is regarded by everybody as being sick and practically without hope. Instead, he needs above all to be listened to, and the state of grace evoked by the secret garden allows Mary to experiment with this new possibility.

Openness

In the novel, unveiling a mystery goes along with discovering relationship. The basic attitude is the same: the position of *openness*. Being open to novelty is being open to encounter. It is the gesture of turning towards otherness, and holding it in our own experience. Rollo May has caught the core of this process, describing a fancied encounter between an artist and his object.

"Cézanne sees a tree. He sees it in a way no one else has ever seen it. He experiences, as he no doubt would have said, 'being grasped by the tree'. The arching grandeur of the tree, the mothering spread, the delicate balance as the tree grips the earth – all these and many more characteristics of the tree are absorbed into his perception and are felt throughout his nervous structure. These are part of the vision he experiences. This vision involves an omission of some aspects of the scene and a greater emphasis on other aspects and the ensuing rearrangement of the whole; but it is more than the sum of all these. Primarily it is a vision that is now not tree, but Tree, the concrete tree Cézanne looked at is formed into the essence of the tree. However original and unrepeatable his vision is, it is still a vision of all trees triggered by his encounter with this particular one" (May, 1975: 77-8).

According to May, the creative act is wholly contained in this encounter. We may go further, and consider how such an experience of openness and encounter is possible in our everyday life too. According to Martin Buber, artist's vision transforms the encounter with the object in a new object in itself, which promotes a new encounter, which is with the observer. This transformation is possible uniquely if it is based on a deep feeling which is our most human quality; it stands indeed at the very root of our being relational creatures. Let us read Buber's own words:

"I see a tree.

I can get it as an image: motionless pillar in the light's dazzling radiance, or bright green crossed by the mildness of the silvery blue background. I can perceive it as motion: the flowing of the grain upon a steady and longing core, the sucking of the roots, the breathing of the leaves, infinite exchange with earth and air – and the dark growth itself.

I can classify it in species, and observe it as a specimen, in accord with the way it is made and how it lives.

I can put aside its peculiarity and the way it is made, up to the point of acknowledging it only as an expression of the law – those laws by which a continuous opposition of powers continuously reconnects, or one of those laws by which the material elements are united and divided.

I can damn it and immortalize it in ciphers, in the pure numeric relationship.

With all this, the tree remains for me an object, an object in space and time, with its ways and its features.

However, by will and by grace together, it can happen that, observing the tree, I become involved in a relationship with it, so the tree is no more an 'it'. The power of exclusiveness has seized me.

To this, it is not necessary for me to give up my ways of observation. There is nothing that I should neglect seeing, in order to see it, nor any knowledge that I should forget. Rather, it is all together there, image and motion, kind and specimen, law and number, indivisibly united.

All that pertains to the tree is there together, its shape and its mechanisms, its colours and its chemistry, its conversing with elements and with the stars, all in one wholeness.

The tree is not an impression, neither is a game of my imagination, nor is a mood, but rather a living body in front of me, and it has to do with me, just like I have to do with it, only in a different way.

Don't try to weaken the significance of relationship: relationship is reciprocity" (Buber, 1923: 62-3).

Buber calls this way of meeting otherness: "the fundamental word I – Thou", which founds the world of relationships. How many times, in our adult life, had we had these kinds of feelings? How many times have we felt so open to the world and encounters? Perhaps, not too many; yet, if we think about it, we realize that each of them has a story that is worth being remembered and sometimes told. It happens while regarding a work of art, or a striking view. It happens more often with people, but perhaps it is going to happen less often as we grow. Because, although the potential range of our experiences enlarges, growing old enforces our selective attitude, and our ways to meet the world decrease, as we tend to keep out everything that seems to not give us some advantage. However, if we recall to mind our childhood, we will see that this quality presides over every experience. Walt Whitman wrote:

> "There was a child went forth every day,
> And the first object he look'd upon, that object he became,
> And that object became part of him for the day or a certain part of the day,
> Or for many years or stretching cycles of years".
> (*There was a Child Went Forth*)

We can learn a lot looking at children. I discovered anew the delight of watching the moon as I witnessed the first encounter of my little daughter with that shining wonder adorning our sky for free every night.

Trust

The possibility itself of an explorative stance, even if we call it an instinct or, using less obsolete words, an inborn behavioural pattern, is strictly tied, in humans, with another element, both symmetrical and complementary to it. I have defined this element with the general term of *trust*. If exploration implies the risk of getting lost, I can explore an unknown land only if I am aware of the way back. Children can open themselves to the world only if the point of departure is firm and safe. John Bowlby has been dealing at length with this point, putting together his clinical observations with theories and models of both psychoanalysis and ethology. He succeeded in understanding the deep connection between the ways of attachment (to the mother, firstly, but also to other meaningful figures) and children's ability to encounter the world. Bowlby's position provides a new point of view upon the polarity dependence/independence, maintaining that "a safe attachment" is the necessary requirement for people's growth towards a proper fulfilment of their individuality. Therefore, the most important feature of being parents is "providing a secure basis from which children or adolescents can start to reach out to the external world, and to which they can come back, knowing for sure that they will be welcomed, nurtured both on a physical and emotional plane, comforted if sad and reassured if frightened" (Bowlby, 1988: 10). Such a delicate balance between protection and freedom engenders in children a wide feeling of trust, which sustains them in the possibility to explore the external world. Later in life, it will redouble, becoming self-confidence, meaning not only awareness of one's potentialities and resources, but also a basic acceptance of one's own being, and trust in others, which is firstly recognising oneself in others, acknowledging a primary resemblance with other human beings. The acts of trusting ourselves and of trusting others, dialogue with the fundamental gesture of openness: we are born open to the world, and people caring for us have the great responsibility to preserve this openness, feeding it with selfless love. If there is such a dialogue, trust and openness will sustain each other, mutually empowering themselves.

Wonder

However, I am convinced that the most fertile ground of both the principles we have examined stands in the third, more mysterious condition of curiosity: the sense of wonder. It is perhaps the secret poetry of childhood, which many grown-ups regret, which some have tried to find again, and which only a few poets, dreamers and visionaries have been able to tell. Gabriel Garcia Marquez's novel *A Hundred Years of Solitude* is one of the greatest narratives of the last century, in which everyday and supernatural situations are wisely entwined to make up a big fresco of the human condition. It begins with these words: "Many years after, before the firing squad, Colonel Aureliano Buendia would remember that remote evening when his father took him to meet the ice" (Marquez, 1967: 9).

What is wonder? We can indeed affirm that it has an emotional connotation. Since Darwin, emotions have been classified in different ways, yet everybody agrees that joy and surprise are among those whose expression is almost universal. Joy and surprise recall to the mind the experience of receiving a gift: if we observe children following a butterfly, or looking at an endless line of ants, we will find the same countenance we saw in them when unwrapping Christmas gifts. Yet the horizon of wonder crosses the border of the mere emotion, and foreshadows a respect towards the things of the world that may take either the form of a contemplative devotion or the form of a yearning to inquire into them. In the world of grown-ups, the places where the discipline of wonder is practised are monasteries, science laboratories, and artists' studios. Certainly, we also have the wonder factories, which comply with our desire to live the condition of a dreamed childhood again, and it happens too that a visionary like Walt Disney turns out to be a multinational. And with a shade of sadness we must admit that this attitude, the most important feature of curiosity, is also the hardest to maintain as adults. Our increasing craving for wonder pairs with a basic inability to wonder, and becomes insatiable starvation: it is the torment of Tantalus of opulent society.

The American psychologist M. Csikszentmihalyi, who had thoroughly interviewed about a hundred eminently creative people, affirms that "practically every individual who has made a novel contribution to a domain remembers feeling awe about the mysteries of life and has rich anecdotes to tell about efforts to solve them" (1996: 156). He adds: "the first step towards a more creative life is the cultivation of curiosity and interest, that is, the allocation of attention to things for their own sake" (ibid: 346)

Openness, trust, wonder: Marina and the other children have discovered a new game. Now, it's a matter of playing it.

6. Versatility

In the introduction of the latest edition of the *I Ching*[13], we can find the following definition: "Versatility *(Yi)* signifies, at the same time, a sudden and unpredictable change, involving difficulties, disorder and upheaval, and the mind's mobility that allows to cope with such a change keeping oneself in harmony with the *Dao*[14]; it also means easiness, lightness, fluidity and openness" (Ritsema-Sabbadini, 1996: 27). The word versatility derives from the Latin word *versor*, which means: being in a specific situation. It is also related to the verb *versare*, which means: turning to, turning around, turning over, and shaking. An intrinsic sense of motion is present in this word. Its contrary is rigidity, which evokes death. If curiosity predispose us to encounter, versatility provides us with the means by which encounter can be alive. It is the possibility of possibilities, and if it entails a sojourn in chaos, we can face it with a smile.

Viewpoint flexibility

This is the first and foremost element of versatility. In creativity literature, since the early Fifties' theories on divergent thinking, the ability to increase the number of hypotheses is regarded as a key feature for triggering the creative processes. We can synthesize this attitude with the word of Edward De Bono, perhaps the most famous inventor and populariser of techniques for boosting creative thinking: "among all creative activities, the most fundamental is the search for alternatives" (1992: 142). De Bono has made popular the metaphor of "lateral thinking", which, contrary to the procedures of linear thinking we normally use to solve problems, takes into consideration all the possible associations, even those that seem rather unlikely. While linear thinking works, so to speak, like a tree, lateral thinking works like a bush. The psychologist Sarnoff A. Mednick, author of one of the most renowned tests on creative thinking (called RAT: Remote Associates Test), points out that creatively gifted people show to have a hierarchy of association which is flatter and more open to change than people less creative. This means that at any given stimulus, the creative person has many more available associations, all with rough probabilities of retrieval (in Rothenberg, 1976: 227-37).

The generation of a variety of interpretations of events, through the activation of novel association patterns, is not only important in solving problems, but also in creating them. While the earlier researches have focussed on creativity as a tool for problem solving, the more

---

13   The *I Ching* (known also as *I King*) is a very old Chinese oracle book. Acknowledged in Western culture for over three centuries (it has influenced Leibniz and his work on binary system), it has become immensely popular thanks to the passionate sponsorship of C.G.Jung. The sinologist Richard Wilhelm, author of the first western edition, translated the title as *The Book of Changes;* a more recent version, by the scholar Rudolf Ritsema, who devoted a thirty-year study to it, is named *The Book of Versatility.*

14   *Dao (Tao)*, is the law of universal harmony, ruling and transcending the conflicts among contraries.

recent ones had underlined how creativity's most precious virtue is its capacity for problem finding, that is giving birth to new questions, without which we can't make progress neither in science nor in the arts.

A very fascinating point in this discussion is the emphasis upon the role of chance in creative processes. The creativity scholar D.K.Simonton openly maintains that creativity works as a stochastic process (in Sternberg, 1999). In statistics, a stochastic process is a sequence in time of random variables. Gregory Bateson has retrieved this notion, in his quest for "the structure that connects" the evolution of living forms with the development of the human mind, and has re-defined it as follows: "stochastic: from the Greek verb *stochazein*, shooting with bow and arrows. That is: spreading the events in a partially random way, so some of them have a favourable outcome. If a series of events combines a random component with a selective process, so only some result of the process can last, such a succession is called stochastic" (1979: 303). Adding that: "creative process must always contain a casual component" (*ibid*: 243). If we have many arrows in our quiver, not only do we have more chances to hit the target, but we may also allow ourselves to make some mistake. And what happens if an arrow is lost in the woods? Which new wonders could we find if we follow it?

The list of important discoveries that have happened almost by chance is endless: from Archimedes' bathtub to Newton's apple, from Galvani's frog to Fleming's mould. To quote a more recent instance, we can think about the discovery of the so called "mirror neurons". The researchers of Pavia University were studying the presence of neuronal systems presiding over movement: some peanuts were placed in front of a monkey, and special equipment recorded the activation of neuronal nets in the animal's brain when it seized them. When a person got near and casually took a peanut from under the monkey's eyes, researchers were astounded to notice that the same groups of neurons were activated, either when the action was actually done by the animal, or when it was only looked at. The initial discovery has lead researcher to investigate more in this direction: the field is still expanding, and further researches, despite the doubts of some members of the scientific community, look very promising (see Rizzolati. Sinigaglia, 2006)[15]. Robert Merton, one of the founders of contemporary sociology, introduced the chance principle in social sciences in the early Fifties, calling it *serendipity*. "The model of *serendipity* refers to the relatively common experience of observing an *unforeseen, anomalous,* and *strategic* datum, which provides the occasion for the development of a theory or the expansion of a pre-existing theory" (Merton, 1968: 255). The word was coined in 1754 by the English novelist Horace Walpole, from a story he remembered to have read, entitled *The Three Princes of Serendip* (one of the ancient names of the isle of Ceylon). Those princes, during their travels, "were always discovering things, by accident or sagacity that they were not in quest of". Although, as Merton shows in his book on the topic, the tale was telling something rather different; the word, however, remained, and in time it has became more and more widespread: in 2001 the web pages found by Google were 636.000 (Merton, 2003: 435); now, in 2006, they are more than 10.000.000! Perhaps, many times the use of the word is due more to its particular music than to its actual meaning. Nonetheless, its success is strictly tied to the growing interest for creativity in the last decades of XX Century, describing a phenomenon that has always been an indispensable component of scientific progress.

---

15   For instance, they may describe what happens in our brain when we recognise the expression of an emotion.

Of course, it takes a trained and ready mind to grasp casual clues and transform them in research projects. Many apples had fallen from trees before the one that offered Newton the idea for his theory of gravity, and a weak adhesive had already been invented in the 3M laboratories, and discarded as a mistake, before Art Fry had used it to invent the *post-it*[16]. The condition of receptivity, that particular flexibility that allows us to suspend the rules to meet the exceptions, to stop the mental schemes that hinder us from acknowledging an unexpected gift, is a form of the attitude we have previously called openness to the world, and, like that, it can be fostered, cultivated, and sustained. Gianni Rodari, the greatest Italian writer for children of the last century, who was a tireless advocate of a creative education[17], has invented the "fantastic binomial", a tool for story-making, using the casual combination of two words coming from different categories. "In the fantastic binomial", he writes, "words are not taken in their everyday meaning, but freed from the verbal chains to which they usually belong. They are estranged, puzzled, thrown against each other in a sky never seen before. So they are in the best condition to generate a story" (Rodari, 1973: 19). With a polite maieutics, the educator Rodari succeeded in rousing in children the vastest amount of possible associations, helping them afterwards to rearrange such association into original narratives.

"Now each of you can write on a sheet of paper, not allowing the others to see, an idea on this title: 'tree and girl'. Who has no idea, will write nothing; but the more people write, the more material we shall get. If you have a foolish idea, even the most stupid idea, write it down" (Rodari, 1981: 38).

Rodari, as a writer, often got inspiration from casual associations. He explains ironically his procedure in the novel *Fantastic Zip Code*. It is an imaginary letter to the Postmaster General, written by an old man who received a booklet containing the zip codes of all the Italian communes, and reads it at night to help him fall asleep.

"Read, read… *Samassi, Samatzai, Sambatello, Sambrusòn…*
It was at that moment that something sprang into me, a spur I've never known, a sudden fruit of intuition, or subliminal perception (you know, that thing that allows one, while asleep, to discover the formula of the oxyribonucleic acid, the deadly ray, and so on). Well, please don't ask me for a scientific description of the mechanism, of the enlightenment that has crossed me, coming from the depths of the space or of the unconscious, either personal or of the human species.
Suddenly, therefore, the sound of *Sambrusòn* evoked another one: the sound – please don't smile – of the word *trombone*".

The old gentleman hastens to explain that he has never had anything to do with trombones; in fact, he never played any instrument, except for a little harmonica in his youth. Unspoiled by self-biographic elements, the link between the two words must be only a matter of sound.

16 The invention of the famous yellow paper sheet has become a little legend. Its inventor, Art Fry, was a technician of 3M, keen on choral singing. He had to cope with an annoying problem: he would put in his missal some pieces of paper as bookmarks, and they would fall down every time he opened the book on the music stand. 'I don't know if it was a dull sermon or divine inspiration, but my mind began to wander and suddenly I thought of an adhesive that had been discovered several years earlier by another 3M scientist, Dr. Spencer Silver' whilst looking for a stronger one. (in Roberts, 1989: 224)

17 'He used to say that it is better to make the school laugh, rather than cry', as one of his pupils remembers (in: Rodari, 1981:18).

"At this point, it became necessary to connect *Sambrusòn* with 'trombone' using something less fragile and perhaps more meaningful than just a rhyme. Who was in *Sambrusòn* (Venice district, zip code 30030) playing a trombone? Why did he play it? Was he a member of the town brass band, of a dance band, or of a rock group? Did he play it for himself, to express his feeling with music? Was he in love? Was he a happy lover or a rejected one? Maybe he was not a simple trombone player, but a teacher, who taught technique, history, and literature of the instrument. And whom did he teach? A boy? A girl? A goat? (…)

Mister Postmaster General, please, believe me: I am in no way responsible for this goat. How she slipped into the series, after all quite rational, of my questions, representing not only her zoological family, but also the family of whim and absurdity, I am not able to explain. She was there, and that's all. If she were a sheep, I could ascribe her unsuitable presence to my habit of counting sheep to fall asleep, although I quitted lately in favour of zip codes. But she was not a sheep: she was a goat. Actually, more than one. I imagined the trombone player crowded by many pretty goats, bearded and bleating, to whom he tried hard to teach how to use the instrument. He was bringing the mouthpiece near to the lips of this and that goat, inviting them to give a blow, just a blow, as he himself would do the rest that is pressing the keys. And the goats, unwilling and absent-minded, ran instead to pluck a tuft of grass, or to kick out a stone. It was clear, too, that the trombone player was not just any amateur or professional, but a goat shepherd, who had learned to play the instrument on his own, just like other shepherds learn to play whistles or reed-pipes, to relieve the boredom of the long hours in the grazing lands. There was only one thing left: to give an accomplished form to the image. So I rose from my bed, took pen and paper, and wrote: *A shepherd from Sambrusòn / was teaching goats to play trombone*" (Rodari, 1993: 638-39).

The process is not, actually, entirely new. In XIX Century, the poet Edward Lear created his *Limericks* from geographical names. The first line introduces a character, tying it arbitrarily to a place: "There was an Old Man of Leghorn". The second line rhymes with the first, and describes a feature of the character from the rhyming word: "The smallest that ever was born". The third and the fourth lines rhyme with each other, developing the above feature: "But quickly snapped up he / Was once by a puppy". The last line ends repeating the name of the place: "Who devoured that Old Man of Leghorn" (Lear, 1970: 148). With this simple structure, Lear populates a bizarre, surprising, and amusing universe. Rodari knew Lear's *nonsense* well, and he himself had made up some of them in the early years of his career as a writer. But his unquestionable genius was in elevating all this to a method, putting it in the more general category of a "fantastic binomial", joining it with a whole range of techniques and procedures allowing children to fully use, nurture and empower their natural versatility of thought. Furthermore, he was a man of strong civil and political passion: he believed that this quality we have called *Viewpoint flexibility* could give a contribution to the education of the citizens of the future, with a critical awareness and a strong inclination towards solidarity. We use our critical awareness when we examine all the possible different interpretations of what goes on, so becoming less incline to take at face value what power and institutions come up with, and more determined to express our opinions and take part in the public choices. Solidarity is when the same stance helps us to "put ourselves in another's shoes", taking into consideration their point of view and understanding their reasons.

This last point introduces us to another fundamental aspect of the element *Flexibility*, concerning the sphere of feelings as well as the sphere of thought. What does it mean, "putting myself in another's shoes"? In interpersonal relationships, this is a delicate and complex process. According to Martin Buber's dialogical philosophy, when I meet another I set up a first, immediate act of identification. The first impulse is mimetic: it is just through this primal mimetic attitude of seeing myself in another that the first bonds are formed in infancy, and I begin to acknowledge myself as being part of a common human heritage (see Pitruzzella, 2003). This first mimetic move of identification is risky: I face the danger of losing myself, of melting entirely with the other, jeopardising those very borders I have established with difficulty through a process of incessant alternation between "mimetic engulfment" and "disengagement from engulfment", in the words of the philosopher Bruce Whilshire (see Wilshire, 1982). My consciousness then withdraws into itself, and starts considering the other in a more objective way: it pronounces what Buber calls "the fundamental word I-It". However, this position barely marks the experience of the other, not the relationship yet. "Relationship is reciprocity"; it can happen when I turn again towards the other and say "the fundamental word I-Thou", which is at the heart of the encounter. In "I-Thou", melting and separation coexist, harmonized in a vital process, like the alternate flowing of systole-diastole in a heartbeat, allowing our continuous interchange with the external world (air filling our lungs and ceaselessly renewing our blood). We can grasp another glimpse of this principle considering empathy. According to Edith Stein (see Stein, 1917), it is slightly different from *sympathy*[18], which means feeling the other's emotion, letting it fill us; vibrating in the unison like the strings of the *viola d'amore*. The prefix *en* (into, inside) instead points to a sense of inclusion: an extension of the range of our experience to contain the experience of the other, keeping us from getting lost in it, but maintaining the sense of ourselves, and eventually putting ourselves at the right distance. This notion has showed itself to be very important in all professions based on what is called a "helping relationship".

We lingered on the element of *viewpoint flexibility* because, as we saw, it is universally considered as a basis for developing creative attitudes. A clear testimony of this potentiality in children is their ability to use objects metaphorically, for example associating them with images through formal or functional analogies. The art historian E.H.Gombrich gives us a delightful illustration evoking the thrill of riding a broomstick that many of us have experienced in childhood. The stick does not resemble a horse: it stands for a horse in virtue of its being suitable for riding. This is for Gombrich the core of artistic acts: representation, not as in imitation but as in standing for (see Gombrich, 1968). Children are able to reconnect and overlap two different frames of reference. The concept of *frame*, enunciated by Bateson and developed by Erving Goffman studying social relations, is the analogue in everyday life of what we call "paradigm" in scientific thought: a set of connections among the elements of a context, which defines it and makes it more comprehensible. We will reflect further upon it later, considering humour. The risk of frame making is to construe self-referential frames, systems folded around themselves. On the one hand, they saturate a need for safety in interpreting the situations where we are; on the other hand, they hinder the possibility of different interpretations, which may happen as we put a single object or event into a different frame. Like Rodari's "freed words", "stick" and "horse" get out from their frames provisionally and meet in play, the land where everything is possible, even crossing over Aristotle's tragic

---

18   From the Greek *sun* (with, together with) and *patheia* (what is felt, good or bad, in body or in morale).

truth: "A is not Not-A": "A child is pretending to be an archbishop. We can use two different verbal forms. We can say 'he is not really an archbishop' and 'he is really an archbishop'" (Bateson, 1956: 34). Dramatherapist Robert Landy adds: "a child playing doctor is both the child (not doctor) and the doctor (not child) at the same time" (Landy, 1995: 8).

The ability to create this kind of connections is visible also in the way children build language. I remember my son, in his first attempts to speak, had coined a series of words to indicate toys and games: the swing was "dindon", suggesting the repetitive movement by evoking the sound of bells; the ring-a-ring-a-roses was "dondo", which sounds like "tondo" (round). When, in his first day at the kindergarten he saw a little merry-go-round, he suddenly called it "dindondo", with a perfect poetic act. As we mentioned poetry, I would like to end this section on flexibility with the voice of a great poet, Gerard Manley Hopkins, who praised the beauty of creation just for its variety:

> "Glory be to God for dappled things –
> 　　For skies of couple-colour as a brinded cow;
> 　　　　For rose-moles all in stipple upon trout that swim;
> Fresh-firecoal chestnut-falls; finches' wings;
> 　　Landscape plotted and pieced-fold, fallow, and plough;
> 　　　　And all trades, their gear and tackle and trim.
>
> All things counter, original, spare, strange;
> 　　Whatever is fickle, freckled (who knows how?)
> 　　　　With swift, slow, sweet, sour, adazzle, dim;
> He fathers-forth whose beauty is past change:
> 　　　　　　Praise him".

(*Pied Beauty*, 1877)

However, multiplicity may also be upsetting. If blind men meeting an elephant in the Indian tale were a single person, he or she would be for sure seized by panic. What is this thing before me? A house, a forest, a rock or a serpent? Most of all: should I fear it? And, well, Pavlov's dog, which was conditioned to react in different ways to different visual stimulations (for instance, wagging its tail to a circle and sitting down to an ellipse), lost heart, and wailed when figures got so similar to become indistinguishable. What it sees is "really a circle" and at the same time "really an ellipse". The trouble is that to the poor beast, trapped in an aseptic laboratory, under the stern gaze of many grim, white-coated humans, has been denied the right to play.

Tolerance

The second relevant aspect of flexibility is *tolerance of ambivalence;* creativity scholars broadly agree its importance as the humanistic psychologist Carl Rogers, who relates it to what we have called *openness*. After having defined openness towards experience as "the opposite of the psychological attitude of defence" (1959: 101), Rogers goes on: "we might say that it means a lack of rigidity and a permeability of the boundary lines in the spheres of concepts, perceptions and hypotheses. We could say that it means a tolerance of ambiguity, where ambiguity exists; which signifies the ability to receive very conflicting information, without forcing the closure of the given situation" (ibid: 102). When facing complex situations, it can be less fatiguing and more reassuring to make use of mental cleavers. The current problem of the confrontation between Islam and the West is a painful example: since the historical, political, social, financial, cultural, and, last but not least, psychological and emotional factors are numberless and extended, it is hard to get a clear and exhaustive picture. It is easier to seek refuge in the cheap metaphor of "civilization clash", which has furthermore the advantage of being a gut feeling, leaving the mind alone. The fact that this will at length intensify the problem instead of solving it, is another kettle of fish.

Moreover, how many times in our lives do we find ourselves obliged to make choices in situations where pros and cons are equivalent, or where we are aware of the presence of conflicting feelings and reasons within us? Sometimes, urged by our own anxiety or by external demands, we choose the first among the solutions at hand, which is not always the best.

I have been using the *I Ching*, the old Chinese oracle book I mentioned before, for many years as an aid to make decisions in tangled situations, and, every now and then, I have also helped people to question it. I preferably apply the procedure with yarrow stems, requiring a long preparation, during which the mind of the questioner is concentrated on the actions of sorting out and counting the stems, leaving aside for a while the horns of the question. And I have a personal idea of the reason why, as odd as it may seem, the oracle undoubtedly works. It is slightly different from the opinion of C.G. Jung, who found in the encounter with the *I Ching* a confirmation of his emergent theory of synchronicity. According to Jung, "synchronicity considers a coincidence of events in space and time as a signifier of something that is more than mere chance: namely, of a peculiar mutual interdependence of objective events, regarding both the observer and their subjective (psychic) conditions" (Jung, 1948: 14). Well, I have no doubt that the category of causality is inadequate to explain all the things in heaven and earth, and that there are connections among things, which are unknown, and probably will remain hidden forever. However, I am also convinced that this is not the only key to understanding the oracle's mysterious effectiveness. When we ask a question, we are usually in a situation in which different interpretations of reality coexist: a potentially creative situation. Yet the difficulty of choosing distresses us, creating a vicious circle: the more anxious we are, the more the possibilities mix up, bewildering us. Questioning the oracle suspends momentarily this vicious circle; its sentences, however, are never clear or direct, and each of them refers to a general picture, whose wisdom is inscribed in the continuous change of things, and their continuously being born. We do not find answer to our questions, but new questions, which enlarge the horizon of the problem, rather than reducing it, so they escort us in uncertainty, and help us to bear it and defer the choice. This allows us to give ourselves the time to listen with freedom and lightness to our inner voice, which is our most profound wisdom. Perhaps the greatness and the unfailing usefulness of *I Ching* lie in the fact that it is a practical training for tolerating ambiguity.

Abraham Maslow, considered the forefather of humanistic psychology, pushes the principle stated by Rogers further: for him, tolerance of ambiguity is a trait of all psychologically healthy people. "Our healthy subjects (…) not only tolerate what is ambiguous and unstructured, but they like it" (Maslow, 1954: 254). He goes on:

"As for healthy people what is unknown is not frightening, they don't need to waste time after procedures intended to protect them from imaginary dangers. They do not disregard the unknown; they do not deny nor escape it; they do not try to pretend that it is already known; they do not organize, or divide it, and they do not pigeonhole it prematurely. They do not clutch for something familiar, their search for truth is not a breathless need of certainty, safety, definiteness and order (…). When the situation as a whole demands it, they can feel at their ease in disorder, chaos and doubt; in uncertainty, indefiniteness, approximation; in what is incorrect and inaccurate (in some moments of science and art or in ordinary life, such things are quite desirable). So it happens that what is doubtful, what is admitted to be a trial, what is uncertain, therefore the necessity of not making a decision (necessity that for many is agony), can be stimulating, can be something higher in their life, instead of being depressing" (ibid: 255).

The most singular paradox of ambiguity is that, from a subjective point of view, it practically does not exist. The neurobiologist Semir Zeki maintains that "in its neurological definition, ambiguity is not the vagueness and uncertainty we find in dictionaries, but its exact contrary: it is certainty, it is indeed certainty of many different interpretations, each of them being in charge for a second. So a definitive answer does not exist, for all answers are plausible" (in: Testa, 2005: 25). For instance, when we see ambiguous images, the focus of perception shifts repeatedly from one area of the cerebral cortex to another. This continuous motion can be source of stress: more than one person says they get a headache from watching reversible pictures (as Escher's stairs, Vasarely's "kinetic pictures", or even the simple sketch of a transparent cube). All in all, ambiguity engenders tension; to bear it, we need to be well equipped. And play is the best training, namely free children's play.

The eclectic French thinker Roger Caillois has called it *paidia,* describing it as marked by "a common principle of fun, of turbulence, of free improvisation and of a light-hearted vital wholeness" (1967: 29); it is different from *ludus,* which involves preset rules, as in games. Many experimental studies seem to agree that there is a close connection between free play and the ability to conceive different interpretations of the same reality. For example, in an experience led by Prof. J.L. Dansky of Eastern Michigan University, some common little objects (such as clips, empty boxes and paper cups) were given to two homogeneous groups of children. Children of the first group were free to play with the objects, as they liked; the other group was invited to play imitative games with the same objects. A third control group was provided with coloured pencils and asked to colour some drawings having nothing to do with the above objects. At the end, after about ten minutes of activity, each single child was asked to think about any alternative use of those objects. As it was expected, children who had free played were proposing many more possibilities to use the objects in a much more unusual and original way rather than the in other two groups, whose answers were quite similar (Runco, Pritzker, 1999, vol. 2: 401). The space of play is where different interpretations of reality can coexist, always forming new possibilities.

However, the issue of tolerance of ambiguity becomes more meaningfully critical when different interpretations are so incompatible that they come into conflict within us, generating a painful impasse. Feelings, emotions, and opinions clash on our soul's battlefield, leaving us at times speechless, defenceless, and frightened. Yet conflict is somewhat inherent to our very humanness. Erich Fromm, a psychologist on the border between psychoanalysis and humanistic psychology, reminds us of the primal conflict of human beings, between "the fact that we are tied to the animal kingdom with our body, its needs and its ultimate destruction, and the fact that, at the same time, we transcend animal nature in virtue of our self-awareness, our imagination and creativity" (Fromm, 1959: 75-6). It is the big topic of Buddhism, that of the *impermanence*: the awareness of our unavoidable decay and end, and, together, the duty of living, the necessity to give any meaning to our existence. And our brief passage in this world is crossed by other huge conflicts, that our ancestors had always expressed as a struggle between principles or gods: Darkness and Light, God and Satan, Good and Evil, up to its final radical incarnation in the fight between Eros and Thanatos, in the last vision of Freud, embittered by the miseries of war and incline to pessimism. Yet conflict is what preserves us from stillness and inertia: "Without contraries there is no progress", says one of William Blake's "Proverbs of Hell" (from *The Marriage of Heaven and Hell*). Quoting again Fromm, "conflicts are the source of wonder, of development of strength, of what was once called "temper". Who avoids conflicts, becomes a machine working without a hitch, in which all emotion are immediately smoothed and settled, in which all desires become automatic and all feelings are crushed" (Fromm, 1959: 75). A generation later, the Jungian psychoanalyst Aldo Carotenuto echoes: "(conflict) establish itself as the abode of the emergent creative process. Abode means to be inherently cast into the conflict, and knowing how to inhabit it. We must therefore think that one of the fundamental requirements for creative people is the ability to live with conflict" (1991: 587). Living with conflict, facing it in every moment, is our existential mission: only if we accept it we are able to transcend it, and come to an overall vision where darkness and light coexist, a point from where we can celebrate both our limits and our endlessness.

Humour

This is the third relevant aspect of flexibility we want to discuss; we will see how it complements the two former aspects. However, beforehand we will try to define provisionally its domain.

The first association is with laughing. Laughing is universally considered a healthy phenomenon. The Italian singer and comedian Enzo Jannacci ironized as follows: "a good laugh heals everything, even cancer. Oh, yes!" It was not long before physicians would start to popularize the benefits of laughing, and before "laugh therapy" would become a common practice (sometimes with more than a shade of business). I will not insist on this, except to underline that there are so many different ways of laughing, and "laughing with" has not the same value as "laughing at", not only on a moral level, but also as regards to the psycho-physical effects.

In a 1952 conference, Gregory Bateson drew attention to the fact that "among all our everyday behaviours, laughter is one of the three which are commonly connected with convulsive phenomena. The other two are deep grief and orgasm" (Bateson, 1952: 4). He added: "inability for weeping, and decrease of orgasm and laughter, are some of the indicators of illness, which are usually searched by psychiatrists. If they work, it is likely that the individual's state is not so bad. If one of them is instead hypertrophic, or if two or three are reduced or absent, the psychiatrist acknowledges that something is not going as well as it should" (ibid: 5). The complete lack of laughter is nearly always symptom of depression; yet laughing continually is often sign of a severe form of schizophrenia. Thus, we cannot affirm for sure that laughter has per se a positive value, in the making of the person and in their balance. However, it is reasonable to think that the potentially positive qualities of laughter are strengthened when it is sustained by humour, which is to be considered a crucial tool for surviving, even if its actual result is just a smile.

Let us pay one more call to the children's world. I would like to tell you a little story: the story of the first Homeric laughter of my daughter Viola, about six-months old. I was standing with my wife in the front garden, having a conversation about something. Viola was in her mummy's arms, looking around, apparently not interested in the discussion. Down on the ground, Camillo, a funny half-Pomeranian puppy with long pointed ears, was attempting to catch some remains of food from the bottom of a big saucepan. In doing so, he thrusts into the pan his whole head, which disappears, then he takes it out to gnaw a bit of food, and then he puts it again, almost rhythmically. The child stares at him for a little while, then she suddenly bursts into such hearty and contagious laughter that we cannot help stopping the discussion and laugh with her.

What happened? For sure, it was not the first time we had seen Viola laughing. The playing of smiles in first infancy is the first emotional training for children (and mothers too). This is true either assuming that smile is born as an expression of feeling, or considering it as being developed from a simple reflex of satisfaction, becoming eventually, in mother's mirror, a tool of "affective tuning"[19]. There are other interplays between mother and infant that are likewise tools of affective tuning, although they provoke laughter rather than smile, like peek-a-boo and tickling. Yet they work in a different way than a smile. While smiling develops along a pattern of continuous mimetic play, laughter explodes from sudden discontinuities, acting as a release from the tension produced by the play itself. In tickling, children laugh not because of the physical effect of touch, which should ordinarily result in some body twisting, but because they perceive a mock attack. Similarly, in peek-a-boo, the anxiety for the disappearance of the mother, evoking a deeper fear of loss, is exorcised in a play of being-not being. Laughter springs from the clash of two conflicting experiences of the world: risk and safety, just as in another game, likewise exhilarating: throwing the baby in the air and grabbing them down again (this is actually a more daddy-style game).

The spark of laughter goes from two different polarities; permit me to add that this involves a very early recognition of the "as if" frame, which, according to Dramatherapy theories, is a unique human quality, by which we may say we are all "dramatic creatures". I think that with these examples we got nearer to the core of humour. Its dynamics have been variously described. Bateson, in the conference quoted above, spoke about the relation between figure and background (in Gestalt terms): laughter is triggered by a sudden reversal of the two. Arthur Koestler, in *The Act of Creation*, a book that has become willy-nilly a classic of creativity, has a more inclusive position. He maintains that at the root of humour there is "the perceiving of a situation or idea in two self-consistent but habitually incompatible frames of reference" (Koestler, 1964: 35). He uses the term "matrix bisociation", where matrix means "any ability, habit, or skill, any pattern of ordered behaviour governed by a 'code' of fixed rules" (ibid: 38).

In every act of humour, such a singular match is present. It is very clear in jokes, where a frame carefully built suddenly crashes at the entrance of another one (and it is not a case that many jokes are based on double entendres). It is present in countless witticisms and puns: when Woody Allen says: "God is dead, Marx is dead, and I am not feeling too good either", we hear

---

19   See Stern, 1985: 147 *passim*

the bizarre creaking of two parallel universes, the one of great ideas and values, and the one of everyday little miseries. Among the thousands of drama games invented by Keith Johnstone, an improvisation genius, there is a game that I find invaluable to create an atmosphere of healthy and convivial fun. In it, two actors are on stage, each of them having the instructions of moving within his/her reality, denying the other's, yet continually interacting with the other. An example: "A – Er…Are you waiting for Percy?; B – Who's Percy?; A – What are you doing here then?; B – I' waiting for a bus.; A – A bus?; B – Where else should I wait?; A – In my living room?; B – Get out of the road!; A – Take your hands off me!; B – That truck nearly hit you!; A – Look at you. You're trampling mud all over the carpet.; B – You're mad!; A – And you are trespassing!; B – Trespassing?; A – I'm phoning the police!; B – Oh, you're one of those confounded mimes!; B – A mime?; A – Well, you're using a mimed telephone. And so on, until they exit in rage, or until one gets sucked into the other's reality" (Johnstone, 1979: 103-4). Lastly, in J.K.Rowlings' Harry Potter novels, the dissonance between the wizards' world and the worlds of *Muggles* is the source of an endless series of gags and jokes.

According to Koestler, the "matrix bisociation" is at the very root of any form of creativity: humour, artistic and scientific creativity. One may not agree with such a generalization, but cannot help appreciating the author's wit when he states that creative acts manifest themselves in the "aah" of art, the "aha" of science and the "haha" of humour.

Going back to the story of Viola's laughter, we can add that the levels of bisociation are manifold. On one level, there is peek-a-boo, which itself is a bisociation between risk and safety, a negotiation between the restlessness of absence and the relief of presence, within the play frame. On another level, there is the odd fact that who plays peek-a-boo is Camillo the dog! Furthermore, the parents' laughter was not only resounding with sympathy: it was enough to put ourselves in her shoes to get the funny side of the matter, the overlapping of the human universe (mummy-daddy-baby-peek-a-boo) with the animal one (Camillo-dog-food). After all, it is the same intuition of Walt Disney in the XX Century, Grandville and Daumier in XIX, and earlier, to Aesop and perhaps further.

Being founded upon the coexistence of different frames, humour is a form of versatility, so it is a basic part of creativity. The neuro-psychologist V.S. Ramachandran seems persuaded of this, when he writes: "the ability to see familiar concepts from new perspectives (which is an essential element of humour) can be an antidote to conservative thinking and a catalyst for creativity. Laughter and humour are perhaps the dress rehearsal of creativity, and, if so, jokes, puns and other forms of fun should be introduced very soon in primary school's programs" (Ramachandran, 1998: 232).

We have discussed the approach to play, and its dynamics; now, let us try to consider the ways of being within the play.

7. Presence

Reflecting on children's play has allowed us to begin exploring the constellation of traits forming the creative personality, with the help of the words of many who inquired into the concrete manifestations of creativity in individuals, trying to extract some general principles. A clearer picture comes out of the role creativity plays in our development as persons and in our experience of the world.

With *Curiosity*, we have investigated a certain way to turn towards the world, to meet experience - an *open* way, contrasting the *closed* ways of indifference and withdrawal.

With *Versatility*, we have investigated a way to consider the world, to be exposed to experience - an *open* way, contrasting the *closed* ways of thought rigidity and emotional stiffness.

With *Presence*, we will examine a way of being in the world, to live experience. This examination will be undoubtedly more complex, as the issue more elusive. If the first two of those we have called "the emblems of creative process", share the feature of being visible to an observer, this condition of experience we defined as *Presence*, can be described almost only from within, therefore it seems to possess some quite indefinable, though fundamental, qualities.

Rollo May wrote: "Terms like 'absorption', 'getting totally seized', 'deeply concentrated' and other analogues are commonly used to describe the condition of the artist or of the scientist in a creative moment, or even that of children playing" (in Anderson, 1959: 85). Observing children immersed in play, we perceive their absorption straightway, their temporary cutting out the rest of the world, and a loving devotion to the little world continuously bred through play. Sometimes I was a discreet witness to my daughter's play with her dolls or her felt animals (other times she involved me as a playmate). It occurred quite often for a rather long period, starting when she was about three years old until now, when she is nine. Of course, along such a span, I noticed an improvement both in complexity and in aesthetic sense of the stories she was staging with her toys, as well as a heightened awareness of her role as a "maker of worlds", voicing many characters and developing with them intricate plots, sometimes intervening as a "deus ex machina": dramatist, director and actress in the meantime. Yet, from the first elementary dialogues of the beginning to the latest complex adventures, what was not changing was her capacity to delve completely into the play, barely noticing my presence. It even happened that I had to call her two or three times, before she noticed me (she quickly restored her concentration after the interruption, resuming the story just at that point: this shows how such a state of absorption is, for children, easy and immediate to enter).

However, beyond all this, if we listen carefully, we may perceive in children's engrossed play a profound tune, evoking a quality of shining joy, a particular wholeness that had made people look at childhood as a reminiscence of a lost "golden age", which adults may hardly ever glimpse, except artists, wise people, and fools. And only poets have attempted to put it into words.

We will try to approach respectfully this quality through the exploration of three more keywords: *Intensity, Attention* and *Aesthetic sensitivity*.

Imagine yourself having a piece of clay in your hands. You will probably do a cursory examination, estimating its size, weight, and consistency. Then you will go on pursuing the purpose you may presume clay is for: making objects. Unless you have been given precise instructions to explore the material in every possible way and using all the senses, your experience of clay will be mostly based on pre-existing categories. Marina and her friends experiment instead with it, letting the clay itself lead the game, building with it an experience of dialogue. "Experience", according to John Dewey, "is the result, the sign, and the reward of that interaction of organism and environment which, when is carried to the full, is a transformation of interaction into participation and communication" (Dewey, 1934: 22). From his specific point of view, Dewey takes us back to the theme of encounter and relationship as discussed before, which will reappear later in this book in various forms. We may synthesize it with the formula: "every true experience is the experience of an encounter", because only within the horizon of encounter experience ceases to be a mere sum of perceptive data and becomes sense, and, in its being sense, offers itself to be incorporated in the process of making ourselves as persons.

In Arts Therapies practice, the free exploration of the expressive media, which is the analogue of Dewey's "interaction of organism and environment", is preliminary to the construction of this quality of experience. For instance, the first part of the Dramatherapy process (which I have called *Foundation*[20]), is set around playing with the elements of drama: tools (body, voice and speech; objects) and structures (the "as if" frame, narrative and roles). It is like what Carl Rogers defined "the ability to amuse oneself with elements and concepts", seeing it as one of the main traits of the creative personality. Above all, it is important because it shapes and supports this particular attitude towards experience. How does the entity of experience, where "interaction turns into participation and communication" manifest itself in the dramatic process? This question is worth a little digression.

The dramatic process, like all complex ones[21], it is not a progressively accumulative process, but it is rather punctuated by special moments which mark discontinuities and qualitative leaps.

These special moments are often turning points in the journey undertaken by both the individual and the group within the *dramatic reality*[22]. They are often connected with deep personal insight of the participants; the metaphoric mirroring of the inner world of the person in the world of drama allows an acknowledgement of the former through the latter; people can give names to this understanding, endowing it with meaning according to the knowledge each one has of themselves. Yet just as often, it is simply experienced, with emotional intensity certainly, but without conscious elaboration. At times, it is even harder to put it into words, and it can be partially expressed only in a symbolic way, through other non-verbal media.

Nevertheless, it works. After these events, people show undeniable signs that "something has changed". They are more relaxed, more open to communication and relationship; they seem to enjoy more the things they do. Often these signs are also visible in the "external world", in people's everyday life, and they foreshadow further lasting transformations. Usually

---

20 See Pitruzzella, 2004
21 On complex processes, see Bocchi /Ceruti, 1972
22 The concept of *dramatic reality* is thoroughly exposed in: Grainger & Duggan, 1997; Jennings, 1998

they are visible thresholds in the growth of people's dramatic abilities. This opens us to the possibility that the dramatic process can reach further healing steps.

During these moments, it almost seems that a multitude of fragments scattered along the way in the previous dramatic work suddenly take on a visible form, often in the shape of symbolic structures.

The dramatherapist can recognize these fragments, and trace some of the threads connecting them. He/she can try to understand and explain the sense of the event, and can even hope for it and help induce the conditions in which it can happen; however, the event itself always occurs as a sudden epiphany, engendering surprise and wonder in the therapist too.

In all the Dramatherapy groups that I have led in the last ten years, I have come upon events of this kind. Usually, participants immediately recognize them as important moments, and remembered distinctly and in detail. In a certain sense, they are "crucial scenes" of the collective drama developing in the Dramatherapy process. I have called these events "states of grace" (see Pitruzzella, 2002).

Intensity

In reflecting upon the *states of grace,* I found an intriguing assonance with what Mihaly Csiszentmihalyi has called *Flow.* The American psychologist has investigated for quite a long time the meaning and value of the "optimal experiences", those moments when "instead of being buffeted by anonymous forces, we do feel in control of our actions, masters of our own fate. On the rare occasions that it happens, we feel a sense of exhilaration, a deep sense of enjoyment that is long cherished and that becomes a landmark in memory for what life should be like" (Csiszentmihalyi, 1990: 3). He concluded that such experiences are at the very root of happiness. Although they are placed in very different domains of action (the author has begun studying artists, athletes, musicians, chess masters and surgeons, then extending his research to many other categories), it seems that these experiences are lived and told in very similar ways.

The first characteristic is implicit in the statement itself, and involves the difference between pleasure and enjoyment. While the first term refers to a situation where our need and desires are fulfilled, the second has a larger breadth, transcending the mere strengthening of the ego: a feeling that goes beyond satisfaction and leans on the unexpected, owning a quality of novelty and wholeness. In this condition, people live a singular paradox: they are extremely concentred in action, and, at the same time, they have the sensation of "being in flow", where effort is not anymore felt and time vanishes. Perhaps William Blake was referring to something alike, when he was writing: "the Time it has taken in writing was thus render'd Non Existent & an immense Poem Exists which seems to be the Labour of a long Life all produc'd without Labour or Study" (Letter to Thomas Butts, April 25: 1803).

According to Csiszentmihalyi, the emotional state arousing *Flow* experiences is a correct balance between boredom and anxiety. If the task we face is too easy for our level of competence, we will be pray to tedium or impatience, or we will continue doing it as a mindless routine; if it is too difficult, anxiety will prevail, triggered by fear of going wrong and from a sense of inadequacy, and we might even give up. When, on the other hand, the challenge is engaging and suitable for our forces, all our energies will focus towards the same direction, defying the "psychic entropy", which lies at the root of our discontent. However, the author warns that even the concentration should not be too outbalanced: "Attention disorders and stimulus overinclusion prevent flow because psychic energy is too fluid and erratic. Excessive self-consciousness and self-centeredness prevent it for the opposite reason: attention is too rigid and tight" (Csiszentmihalyi, 1990: 85). We will return later on the attention issue.

When the experience of *Flow* comes about, it is an "autotelic experience", finding its purpose in itself (from the Greek prefix *auto-*, meaning self-, and *telos*, meaning aim and purpose). Its quality is not based on the expected outcome, but on the action itself: the joy we experience in being in the heart of the process. Yet in the Indian *Bhagavad Gita*, Lord Kṛṣna advises prince Arjuna:

"Be involved only in action, never being interested with the fruits. (...) Complete your actions, Arjuna, being so firm in the yoga, having abandoned the attachment. Be equal in the success and in the failure. (...) The one whose deeds are, without exception, devoid of desire's bond, he who offers everything to the renunciation, this is a true wise man!" (*Bhagavad Gita*, II, 49)

We may apply this principle to creativity as a whole. Teresa Amabile, the social psychologist who devoted her life-long research to understanding how creativity works and spreading the benefits of a creative education (see Goleman et al., 1992: 63-76), focuses her attention to the motivation issue in creative processes. She distinguishes "intrinsic motivation" (coming from within the subject) and "extrinsic motivation" (coming from outside), and maintains that the former leads to creativity, while the latter hampers it (see Amabile, 1983).[23] Amabile, who bases her studies not only upon the analysis of great creative people, but also on thorough experimental researches, has lately modified her hypothesis. She added that, given certain conditions, which she calls "synergic", extrinsic motivation it is not an obstacle for the creative process, and can even help it (see Amabile, 1996): in either case, however, it is always intrinsic motivation that is in charge. In other words, the more a process is goal-oriented, the lesser are the probabilities that it is a creative process. Focussing on the future hinders us from fully living the present.

Play, and primarily children's play, is par excellence the most intrinsically motivated sphere of human activity. The purpose of play is nothing but play itself. In his *Homo Ludens*, which remains a seminal book for any reflection on the argument, Johan Huizinga remarks that play, "not being 'ordinary life', is outside the process of immediate satisfaction of needs and desires. It interrupts that process. It introduces in it a provisional action having a purpose in itself, performed for the satisfaction that lies in that performance" (Huizinga, 1939: 12).

When, in children's play, this *Intensity of experience* is limited or absent, it is usually a bad sign: it means that children are having a difficult time (for example, they are worried about something), or that there are developmental problems. Conversely, in healthy children this feature of experience manifests itself in thousands of signs. Peter Slade (the great English educationist who pioneered Dramatherapy), tells us about the appearance of the *Running Play* in seven to twelve year old children (a play which usually occurs in first infancy, when children

---

23   Of course, creativity history is full of exceptions: it is enough knowing that Collodi wrote his immortal *Pinocchio* to repay gambling debts. And the irony master Tommaso Landolfi, who shared the passion for gambling, answered a journalist asking about his sources of inspiration: "Need, dear. *Need makes the old wife trot…*"

acquire the upright position, and then takes a social shape in tag games). Slade maintains that this run is "great art". His account is so poetical that it is worth reading it almost in full:

"At sudden and special moments a child will break for sheer joy into a run, whether acting or dancing. It may not happen very often, but it is like a flash of lighting when at its best" (Slade, 1954: 63-4).

Abraham Maslow, in his remarkable compendium of psychological wisdom entitled *Towards a Psychology of Being*, describes a condition very alike to Csiszentmihalyi's "optimal experiences", emphasizing their spiritual side. The "peak experiences" described by Maslow are indeed on the threshold of the "oceanic feeling" of being part of a whole, which has been recounted by mystics in every time and land. These experiences are not, however, a prerogative of those who follow a spiritual path, either within a formal religion or not. They are rather available to anybody, when "they have fulfilled their fundamental necessities of safety, of belonging, of love, of self-respect and self-esteem, so they are primarily motivated by self-actualization tendencies, which can be defined as a continuous accomplishment of potentiality, of abilities and talents; as achievement of a mission, or vocation, or destiny and so on; as a more thorough knowledge and acceptance of the person's intrinsic nature; as an incessant inclination towards unity, integration or synergy within the person" (Maslow, 1962: 35).

In "peak experiences", according to Maslow, a certain perception of the world prevails, which is not created by our lacks, existential holes and unfinished business, but by our tendency to grow towards the achievement of the wholeness of being. Maslow depicts vividly the difference between these two different levels of existence, envisaging a threshold between two qualities of love, which coexist as potentialities within each of us: selfish love and selfless love. The first, called *D-love* (D is for *Deficiency*), founded on taking, is a void to fill; the second, called *B-love* (B is for *Being*), founded on giving, is a vase overflowing. The cognition of being in selfless love is at the core of "peak experiences", it is humus and nourishment for them. The author lists some features of these experiences: in them there is a feeling of oneness with the object of experience, apart from its usefulness; a total concentration; a sharpening of perception; they are "autotelic experiences" (see above); in them, people undergo a partial loss of the ego and a disorientation of time and space; they have a "flavour of wonder, of awe, of reverence and of humility" (ibid: 51); they are perceived as intimately transforming experiences. I deem that those moments I have defined *states of grace* are in some ways very close to the experiences described by Maslow, and when they occur, people are allowed to experiment (sometimes for their first time) with the way to meet the world we have called *Presence*, a potentiality expressed in children's free and joyous play. We will go on exploring this point taking into consideration the second keyword, *Attention*, which contrasts and completes our reflection on *Intensity of experience*.

Attention

According to the classic definition, attention is a perceptive filter, selecting the information from the environment, excluding some and favouring others. And this matches roughly with the standpoint of common sense: when a teacher rebukes "distracted" children, she is asking them no less than to cut away from their present consciousness a whole series of stimulations, both external (the buzzing of a fly, a classmate's word, a car passing, a picture in the book, a sunbeam across the clouds, a stain on the wall) and internal (thoughts, a tune in the head, hunger, an itching of the leg, the need to pee). In other moments, such stimulations are nothing but the whole and lively perceptive world of children; but this is another story. The ability to make this filter work has been associated with memory (if I am attentive I remember), with efficiency (if I am attentive I work better) and with vigilance (if I am attentive I do not make mistakes). In addition, we can generally agree that an air traffic controller is not supposed to think about tomorrow night's date while giving instructions for landing. Actually, the matter is a bit more complex: you need only to think how the quality of our motivation (either intrinsic or extrinsic) influences our attention. It is harder to keep our attention on an activity we do not like, than rather on an activity that thrills us. Obviously, the balance between boredom and anxiety conditions our capacity to be attentive.

Attention has been commonly linked with the arousal of the central nervous system, coupled with a diffuse stimulation towards the cerebral cortex. This arousal has been studied with various instruments of psycho-physiological measurement (from EEG to *skin potential response*). In arousal states, attention tends to focus, but it follows the cyclic nature of those states, having a peak and a decline. One of the most interesting elements underlined by many creativity researches is the fact that arousal phenomena are sometimes in inverse relation to creativity. In other words, in some moments of the creative process, people experience a low level of arousal while having a high level of attention (Sternberg, 1999: 73-5; Runco & Pritzker, 1999, vol.I: 141-46). This means that there are at least two different kind of attention: focussed attention and diffused attention. Focussed attention is marked by a strong arousal and short length; diffused attention by a low arousal and longer length. Yet in 1912, Sigmund Freud was aware of it, and advised the aspiring psychoanalysts to maintain a "fluctuant attention" during the session. "So you will spare the effort of attention, in which, anyway, you could not persevere for many hours in succession every day, and you will avoid a danger strictly tied to the application of deliberate attention" (Freud, 1912: 533). These dangers consist is following personal expectations and inclinations in selecting the client's material, and disregarding further unconscious material, which might be just as meaningful. This kind of attention is not selective but uniform, therefore ready to grasp the new and the unexpected (the old story of the psychoanalyst falling asleep during the session is no more than a joke).

Oddly enough, this kind of attention, although fundamental for the psychoanalytic technique, and generally in psychotherapy, has not been studied in detail. To continue with our discussion we must refer to another trend of studies, somewhat recent, yet rooted in an age-old tradition. I would like to start this exploration with a personal story.

I will never forget the feeling of true astonishment of my first encounter with meditation. I was in my twenties and I had the chance to attend a summer camp of the *Communauté de l'Arche,* a non-violent community founded in France, just after World War 2, by an Italian disciple of Gandhi, Giuseppe Lanza del Vasto. This community is founded upon a harmonious blend of Christian heritage and oriental wisdom. One of its rules is the daily attendance of yoga and meditation sessions, which are not exactly in the wake of Indian tradition, but they follow faithfully its spirit. I was still a philosophy student then, and I was quite sure that wisdom derived from knowledge, and that gaining knowledge called for a great effort of mental concentration. Actually, I knew almost nothing at all about meditation. From the little I had heard, I had a hazy expectation: a strong discipline of attention towards some weighty issue, and the eventual discovery of some sort of truth about it. Perhaps, a new truth, something to nurture my restless spirit more than philosophy, which, apart from a few exceptions, had started to reveal itself as an arid intellectual exercise.

Instead, I found myself into something completely different. It is a bit like the difference between going up and down a steep slope. When you climb, you start from a static position, and you must find a standing point to lift yourself up, challenging gravity. When you go down, it is another kind of effort: gravity force helps you, but you have to find a solid place to stop. The teacher asked us to sit down in a comfortable position, with our spine straight, and put all our attention on breathing, just on the air going in and out of our lungs. Obviously, all we neophytes found it outrageously hard to concentrate upon something as trivial as breathing, so our attention was roving around, caught by the sounds of the surroundings (we were in a farmyard), by our own thoughts, and even by the uneasiness of the position itself, hard to keep for long. I began to feel doubtful that I could succeed in the exercise: the harder I tried to follow the rhythm of breathing, the more the rest distracted me. It reminded me of a novel I read as a child (which I later discovered as being the modern version of an old Indian tale), about a stone having the power to transform lead into gold, only if people doing the operation did not ever think about white bears. Of course, nobody could help thinking about them, or thinking not to think about white bears, which is the same. Probably something similar was happening to other people who, like me, were approaching such thing for the first time.

However, it was in that very moment, while we were so discouraged, that the teacher started to speak again. Everything that happens, he said, happens: all your thoughts, all the perceptions of your senses, and even your bodily sensations, are not to be put aside. Allow yourself to observe them like you look at clouds playing in the sky, neither ignoring them, nor concentrating a lot on them. You are aware of all this just like you are aware of your breathing, and you repeat to yourself: I am present. This was exactly what we were doing; yet being aware of it, or rather being aware of our own awareness, apart from its contents, and at the same time being aware of those very contents with a quiet detachment, was a totally new experience. There were thoughts, perceptions and feelings, but they were not thought out, perceived, or felt: they were there, that's it. And there was breathing. I was feeling I was entirely myself, with no need to demonstrate it even to myself. And at the same time, I was experiencing a deep sense of peace and strength. It was only a matter of minutes, but they were enough to let me sense the beauty of this kind of exercise. Later, I was to encounter Buddhism, and began practicing with certain regularity (city life permitting); but first meditation is like first love: you'll never forget it.

"Awareness" is a possible translation of the Pali[24] word *sati*. It is a rather imperfect translation, as awareness implies a specific object: I am aware of something. Using it to tell experiences as such may provoke a word jam, like the one we see above. Another word is more favourably used: *mindfulness*, evoking a "mental wholeness". Under this name, a fruitful trend of research has emerged in the last twenty or so years, experimenting with this age-old practice and understanding its benefits on health, both physical and psychic, and on the creativity of people today.

Buddhism, especially in its older form, presents itself more as a path to heal human beings from their inborn suffering rather than as a religion. Buddha's 'revelation' is not the spreading of a message from a higher Being, but an analysis of human suffering and a

---

24   A language of Southern India, in which the older Buddhist texts are written.

method to go beyond it. The practice of meditation stands at the roots of this method; in the *Theravada* tradition[25] it is mainly *mindfulness* meditation (*Vipassana*). In the late Seventies, an American physician, Dr. John Kabat-Zinn, who had himself practiced various forms of meditation, began wondering if this healing system could fit western medicine. He founded at Massachusetts University a program called MBSR (*Mindfulness-Based Stress Reduction*), aimed at curing a whole range of troubles connected with stress, from psoriasis to panic attacks, from chronic pain to eating disorders. The successes of the program made this kind of intervention multiply, and the practice of *mindfulness* has gained a larger space in the healing field. It crosses various forms of psychotherapy (see Germer, Siegel & Fulton, 2005), either distancing itself from its roots in tradition, thus becoming a specific therapeutic technique (particularly for depression: see Segal, Williams & Teasdale, 2002), or keeping its connections with the Buddhist psychology.

How these approaches understood and applied *mindfulness*? We can start with a commonly shared definition: *mindfulness* is the awareness without judgement of the present moment. It is a condition we can achieve through meditation practice, and consolidate as an attitude towards the world that we can apply to everyday life: living in the moment. This attitude implies "learning to stop all the doing and passing to the mode of being, learning to dedicate time to yourself, slowing the pace down and nurturing calmness and acceptation inside yourself; learning to create space for new ways to face old problems and to grasp the interconnections among all things" (Kabat-Zinn, 2004: 23). It has turned out to be an effective answer to stress, which is the cause of many widespread diseases.

Let us have a short look at some features of *mindfulness* experiences, connecting them closely with creativity, as listed by the psychologist Christopher Germer (see Germer, Siegel & Fulton, 2005: 9). *Mindfulness* is *non-conceptual, present centred, nonjudgmental, intentional, participating, nonverbal, exploratory, and liberating.*

Non-conceptual refers to the shifting of our awareness beyond the process of thinking. Thoughts may come and go, and we can contemplate their genesis and their end, while observing ourselves in the act of making them and eventually losing them, but they are in no way at the centre of our attention, or do they regulate it. *Present centred* refers to the place of *mindfulness*: even if we go with our thought in the past or in the future, we are always here, in this moment and in this body, and we enjoy the pure delight of being. *Nonjudgmental* means that we do not pass judgement on the present moment: it is neither good nor bad, neither right nor wrong, neither useful nor useless. It is here, now, and it is just our moment. *Intentional* refers to the fact that it is not casual but rather wanted (even if there are countless instances of *mindfulness* states presenting themselves in everyday life, though not invoked: in children, I would say, it is almost a regular condition). *Participating* means that we are not detached spectators of it; on the contrary, it implies a passionate approach to an attunement of the body and mind that renews our being people. *Nonverbal* means that it is not manifesting itself in the form of words. We will try to describe it later (as I attempted above), but in the moment it

---

25   Buddhism has many currents, the major ones being: the *Theravada* tradition, now present in Sri Lanka and Indochina, founded on the original teachings of Buddha as written in the Pali Canon: it is quite a laical Buddhism, with a strong psychological orientation; the *Mahayana* tradition, spread in Northern India, which has more a religious-devotional imprint (Tibetan Buddhism, with its own special characteristics, is within this tradition); the *Zen* tradition, philosophic-contemplative, common in Japan but originally born in China by the fusion between the teachings coming from India and the local Taoist tradition.

exists beyond all language. *Exploratory* refers to its quality to be a dynamic experience, rather than a static one, open to all perceptive levels. *Liberating* means that it engenders an immediate sensation of wellbeing (which is often mistaken for mere relaxation).

Of course, the complete practice of Buddhist meditation goes far beyond, towards the attainment of higher spiritual goals. Namely, the non-attachment (acknowledging the precariousness and the impermanence of reality, as we perceive it, to avoid founding the sense of our existence on having) and the compassion (acknowledging the "Buddha nature", the substantial divinity, in all living beings, as in ourselves, and respect it with devotion). It implies a strong and sustained commitment, a thorough study of its principles, with, possibly, an empathic and sensitive guide.

Nevertheless, this first level we call *mindfulness*, is within the reach of everybody, as it is founded upon a quality existing as a potentiality in every individual, and the effort it demands is quite endurable, even for troubled minds.

In creative processes, focussed attention plays its role: when Marina and her friends begin to transform the wonderful little piece of clay into an actual "hocpotus", and making fish, rocks and seaweed to keep it company, they are clearly engrossed in the task. Likewise, any concrete realization (including works of art) demands moments of intense vigilance. However, the specific feature of a creative process is this form of scattered attention, having properties of openness and expansion similar to *mindfulness* experiences, which can be easily retrieved and cultivated.

Aesthetic sensitivity

The quality we have called *Presence* is founded, at this point in our exploration, on two opposite yet complementary pillars, both referring to a mental position, both signals of being entirely in the moment: one is concentration, focussed attention, the other is *mindfulness*, spread attention. Nevertheless, we are not abstract minds: we are throbbing beings, with body and mind united in a unique dynamic organism, in constant relation with the external world. Emotions are involved in the first case, otherwise we would not have our *intensity;* sensations and feelings are involved in the second, otherwise we would not have our *aware attention.* Our relationship with the world occurs through our body and its nerve endings: our sense organs catch fragments of the ceaseless reality stream surrounding us, and deliver them to our mind so it may create an image of the world to live with and to question. This becomes critical in those domains of human experience marked by creativity: art and ritual are cases in point. William Butler Yeats has written: "art bids us touch and taste and hear and see the world, and shrinks (…) from every abstract thing, from all that is of the brain only, from all that is not a fountain jetting from the entire hopes, memories, and sensations of the body" (in Ghiselin, 1980: 107). And the Italian philosopher Elèmire Zolla writes of ritual as "the action tuning music with scents, gestures, and dance positions, visions of sacred colours and shapes (…). The five senses are involved, entwined, and knotted like warp yarns in a loom" (in Fletcher, 1904: XI).

In *Presence,* all the senses play a crucial role: if I think of children playing with clay, I must admit that I had never realized before that a piece of clay has a smell, a taste, and even a sound! Seeing, hearing, touching, smelling, and tasting: it seems quite a trivial fact, but we actually live with a sense apparatus working most of the time at a low speed, idle as it has grown from habit. Everything runs so fast, stimulations come and go one after another, and we seldom linger on them long enough to make them become experiences. Our general sense intelligence decreases; sight prevails and the other senses are underutilized. Just try to imagine how hearing, touch, smell, and taste would work without sight. Try to identify something only by smell or touch, and you will notice how much our senses speak and how little we listen to them. I remember a training experience for primary school teachers, on relating to children with learning disabilities. I was working, among others, with a couple of partially-sighted people, who had proposed a quite singular exercise to the teachers: covering their eyes with special spectacles impeding sight, they had to go out of the school, cross the road (of course with a guide!) and go to a café to drink a coffee. The aim of the exercise was to put oneself in a visually impaired person's shoes, to acknowledge the problems of this condition. What actually happened was that the teachers, after a moment of bewilderment (which, let me say to their credit, never became anguish), noticed a sharpening of all senses, especially hearing and taste (yet some had confessed that they smelt the odour of the coffee 'as if it were the first time'). An introductory exercise to *mindfulness* consists in eating very slowly three raisins, putting one's attention on any sensation evoked (Kabat-Zinn, 2004: 29). William Blake warns us that the experience of "minute particulars" is the main way to encounter eternity: "every Minute Particular is Holy" (*Jerusalem, 69: 42*). He adds: "Art & Science cannot exist but in minutely organized Particulars" (ibid. *55: 62*).

Why so often do "minute particulars" escape us? Because we have no time, we say, unwittingly echoing that character of Saint-Exupéry's *Little Prince* who invented the pill that extinguishes thirst, so people could spare the time to drink (but the Little Prince answers that, if he could spare all that time, he would use it to go slowly slowly to a drinking fountain). In the communication age, the incessant presence of many stimulations, especially visual and auditory, saturates our perceptive capacities, levelling them. Our most primitive senses, taste and smell, tend to fit the standardization of industrial food; even touch is usually underutilized, except for potters, carpenters and few other people (it is clear enough that typing on a keyboard, as I am doing just now, is not at the top of tactile perceptions).

Of course, there is a factor connected with the evolution of species: our cave-dwelling ancestors needed, to survive, much sharper senses than we need. And there is a factor of organization of the perception: the signals that our sense organs receive from the external world are filtered from the central nervous system, controlled by the most archaic parts of our brain (the hippocampus and the limbic system, seat of the emotions), but are elaborated in a special area of the new cortex. The organization of the bare perceptive data can occur either with a *bottom-up* trend (chaos producing order) and with a *top-down* one (order regulating chaos). In the former case, we remain for a while with the perceptions, before giving them a meaning; in the latter case, meaning is the scheme to which perception must conform, leaving the surplus out.

Both the modes of perceptive organization are present in the creative process, though at different moments. However, the special quality of artists is allowing themselves to be surprised by the material they work with, allowing forms to grow organically within a relationship with this material. It is beyond doubt that artists, and, perhaps, all creative people, develop a particular attention to the messages of the senses. Martindale (1999: 144) reports many experimental studies that seem to show that creative people are generally "physiologically hyper-reactive", thus explaining the tendency of many artists to seek seclusion in their productive moments: a temporary withdrawal, which allows an elaboration of their exuberant perceptive world. On the other hand, there are many artists who are inspired by the mixture of different perceptions: Maurice Sendak, the great illustrator of children's books, tells us that his drawings are created with a musical background: "A favourite occupation of mine, some years back, was sitting in front of the record player as though as possessed by a dybbuk, and allowing the music to provoke an automatic, stream-of-consciousness kind of drawing. Sometimes, the pictures that resulted were mere choreographed episodes, imagined figures dancing imagined ballets. More interesting to me, and much more useful for my work, are the childhood fantasies that were reactivated by the music and explored uninhibitedly by the pen" (in Barron, 1997: 130). As for me, I have to confess that part of this book was written under the influence of John Coltrane and Thelonious Monk's jazz music, and I hope this explains my many leaps and lapses.

We all connect different sense perceptions, by virtue of associative processes, ruled by habit, by any causative reason, or just by fantasy; such processes may be even below the level of memory and consciousness. Artists make a systematic use of them. However, there are also people whose connections occur in an immediate, automatic, and powerful way, in the act itself of perceiving. These people, for example, "see sounds": not in the sense told by Sendak, who, listening to Mozart's "dissonance quartet" (the one with "devilish intervals") sketches a carrousel of children, birds, mothers and fish swallowing each other. Proper "synaesthesia" implies a sense evocation lived as a real experience, something that is not "in my mind", but "out there". One of the first thorough descriptions of this faculty is in the classic study *The Mind of a Mnemonist*, by the Russian psychologist Aleksandr Lurija. The prodigious memory of the subject of the study was founded upon a series of synaesthesia, some of which are described in detail:

"A sound of 30 hertz frequency and 100 db intensity is presented. The subject declares to see at first a band of about 12-15 cm in width, of an antique silver colour; gradually, the band gets narrower as if disappearing, and is transformed into an indefinite object, bright as steel. Slowly, the tone takes the aspect of twilight, and the sound continues to dazzle with silvery brightness.

A sound of 50 Hz frequency and 100 db intensity is presented. Š sees a brown band on a dark background with red flames; to the taste, it is similar to sweet and sour boršč (a typical Russian soup), and this sensation expands to the whole tongue.

A sound of 100 Hz and 86 db is presented. Š sees a large band, whose centre is red-orange, gradually shading into pink on the borders" (Lurija, 1968: 30-1).

And so on. Cartoon fans (like myself), might remember the beginning of Walt Disney's film *Fantasia*, fruit of his most "experimental" period (when he was also collaborating with Salvador Dali), where Bach's *Toccata and fugue in b minor* is visually interpreted with a flow of colours on the screen. Lurija comments; "It is now clear that in Š a clear separation did not exist, as in each of us, between sight, hearing, touch and taste. Those synaesthesia, whose traces remain in many ordinary individuals in a rudimental form (that low and high sounds have different colours, that there are 'cold' and 'warm' tones, that 'Monday' and 'Friday' each has its own colour: these are, after all, quite common sensations), were instead persisting in Š as a basic element of his psychic life" (ibid: 33).

Although synaesthesia is an interesting phenomenon, acknowledged by medicine for almost three centuries, it has never been studied systematically. This happened for two main reasons. First, because it is quite uncommon (it has been estimated that one person out of 25.000, with a majority of women and left-handed people, has at least a synaesthetic coupling, which appeared early in their life and is constant in time; yet people with a total synaesthesia, as the one described by Lurjia, are very rare). Second, because it is difficult to be identified with objective criteria: defining exactly the boundary between synaesthesia and imagination is not so easy. The result is that it has been studied mainly when connected with abnormal or even pathological conditions (like the hypermnesy quoted above or the autistic states: see the passionate story of her autistic childhood told by T. Grandin, 1995). Nevertheless, in recent years a fascinating trend of studies has started, suggesting that there are deep and fruitful connections between synaesthesia and creativity, and that Wagner's dream of the "total work of art", which has influenced numberless artists, has its roots in the deepest districts of our mind.

The American neurologist Richard E. Cytowic, who comprehensively studied the issue (see Cytowic, 1989, 1993), holds challengingly that we all are potential synaesthetes. It is obvious that the more evolved part of our brain (the new cortex) is the place where sense information is elaborated and becomes experience: for this purpose, specialised areas for the single senses are located in our brain. However, it is true as well that our brain's plasticity makes these areas have constant intercourses: they interact and they are interchangeable. When, for instance, one of the senses is out of use (as in visually impaired people), the related area is not inert, but 'collaborates' with the other in processing sense information. This may account for the facility with which we can imagine the synaesthetic connections and for the possibility itself of enjoying those forms of art that mingle the senses (otherwise, we could not have either opera or rock concerts). But the most intriguing claim of Cytowic's point of view, derived from observing how in synaesthesia the metabolism of the new cortex drops drastically, is that the core of the matter resides in the most remote areas of the brain, the limbic system and the hippocampus, the mysterious patron of emotions. In plain words: a synaesthete intercepts the perceptive flow before it reaches the sorting areas. The consequent hypothesis is that the process of specialization, which separates the sense perceptions, evolving from the age of four months and continually enhancing until adolescence, in these people has somehow stopped, or it has developed itself in different terms than usual (see Baron-Cohen et al., 1996). Therefore, there has probably been a time in our life where we were in a synaesthetic world, as the perceptive system was undifferentiated. Is it possible that the common person, who has an already differentiated system, can reactivate this synaesthetic potentiality, under certain conditions? On the one hand, I am convinced that this is exactly what happens in the artistic process: artists activate synaesthetic resources drawing them from deep parts of themselves. On the other hand, I think that everyday synaesthesia, those defined by Lurija as "rudimental", often go beyond the mere associations, and are connected with our synaesthetic potential, creative because its virtue can help us to discover new ways to know the world.

On one of these "minor synaesthesia" I have made a little inquiry (a game rather than research). I asked many people in my circle of friends, acquaintances and relatives (both children and adults) the following question: which colours are vowels? It is a rather complex set of associations, of course, as it requires an already made connection between sound and symbol; nonetheless, it is one of the most frequent forms of synaesthesia (see Baron-Cohen et al, 1993). Yet the strongest inspiration for the experiment comes from a poem by Arthur Rimbaud, entitled *Vowels*: it was one of the most "outrageous" works of the young poet who had planned "a long, immense, and reasoned derangement of all senses" as a way to attain the condition of "seer".

The results of the game contain many interesting cues. First, the quite striking fact that for most of the people involved it is not a matter of assigning a colour to the vowels on a precise request, but of reporting something already well known, for many since they were children, and about which there is no hesitation at all. Secondly, the fact that there is a large variety in choices and dominant positions are very limited: A and E have been identified with 7 different colours, I with 11, O with 10 and U with 9. The most frequent associations (A red 41%; E green 51%; I yellow 25%; O brown 19%; U black 27%) are not necessarily correlated: if I see a red A, it doesn't mean automatically that I will see a green E. It seems that, although the association vowels/colours is a rooted and widespread experience, there is not any "synaesthetic truth", even for people with a proper synaesthesia, who, according to the studies, present an analogue variety. Everybody sees them, yet each sees them in his or her own way. And Rimbaud was seeing them in a very special way[26]: two of his associations (A black and E white) are totally absent in this game; I is red for 13% of adults and no child; O is blue for 11% of adults and 9% of children; U is green for 18% of children and no adult. Which secret had the poet discovered in the colour of the vowels, and which shadowy side of the world did he unveil?

> "A Black, E white, I red, U green, O blue : vowels,
> I shall tell, one day, of your mysterious origins:
> A, black velvety jacket of brilliant flies
> Which buzz around cruel smells,
>
> Gulfs of shadow; E, whiteness of vapours and of tents,
> Lances of proud glaciers, white kings, shivers of cow-parsley;
> I, purples, spat blood, smile of beautiful lips
> In anger or in the raptures of penitence;
>
> U, waves, divine shudderings of viridian seas,
> The peace of pastures dotted with animals, the peace of the furrows
> Which alchemy prints on broad studious foreheads;
>
> O, sublime Trumpet full of strange piercing sounds,
> Silences crossed by Worlds and by Angels:
> O the Omega, the violet ray of Her Eyes!"

---

26   "I knew Rimbaud, Paul Verlaine said, and I know that he didn't give a damn if A was red or green. He was seeing them so, and that's all".

8. The creative function

Beginning with an episode of normal creativity in children, we went on exploring the modes of experience that mark creativity and are indeed supporting it: *Curiosity, Versatility,* and *Presence* (see fig. 1). We have seen in detail how such modes of experience work in activating and sustaining the creative processes, and how they can endure and grow steadily as constant personality traits. Such traits are present not only in artists or scientists, serving them to discovery and realization, but even in ordinary people, to whom they may mean an attitude in turning towards the world and towards themselves. Such attitude manifests itself in their ways of coping with small and big life challenges.

Curiosity	Versatility	Presence
Openness	Flexibility	Intensity
Trust	Tolerance	Attention
Wonder	Humour	Sensitivity

Figure 1: The emblems of creative attitude

However, let me return for a while to the discussion upon Arts Therapies I sketched in the Introduction. The Arts Therapies practice has a main and consistent purpose: helping people to overcome the obstacles hindering them from living a whole and meaningful life, whatever the names we give to those obstacles, the metaphors with which we define them, the concepts we construe about their genesis. To do this, we have chosen to use the artistic process. A process intentionally and carefully guided towards its realization, yet undoubtedly a creative process, which allows experimenting personally with the modes of experience above mentioned, and wisely nurturing them.

This is immediately visible in the structures of the artistic process used in the Arts Therapies, which we have defined as *exercise, improvisation,* and *composition*. It is worth keeping in mind that these three structures continually interact along the process: for example, an improvisation may use elements and shapes derived from an exercise; a composition may contain improvised parts; quite often, they are in a sequence: an exercise can include some cues that are developed through improvisation and then organized in a composition. Each of the emblems of creative attitude finds its actualization in all three. To facilitate the exposition, we will try however to recognise their presence in the process starting from each individual structure.

In the *exercise* manner, usually being the opening phase of the process, *Curiosity* is the first to be elicited. People are invited to contact the arts tools through an ongoing progression, eventually leading to a free play of research and experimentation. Taking into consideration the four main disciplines of Arts Therapies (Art Therapy, Dance Therapy, Music Therapy and Dramatherapy), we may group the tools into two large categories, borrowing Peter Slade's distinction of the two major forms of children's play: *projective* and *personal* (Slade, 1954). The use of objects, like paper, colours, and clay in Art Therapy, instruments and sound equipments in Music Therapy, and puppets, masks and props in Dramatherapy, marks out a projective approach. The use of our whole person (our own body in Dance Therapy and in Dramatherapy; in the latter, voice is commonly used too, as sometimes in Music Therapy) marks out a personal approach. Whatever the approach may be, it is always a matter of encounter: we encounter ourselves as beings able to express, communicate and tell, able to give ourselves the permission to play. At the same time, we encounter the tools that allow us to do it. It is also often an encounter with our own limits and impediments, but this does not prevent the exploration of our potentialities, starting from the little we have at hand. In addition, it is an encounter with people: in group Arts Therapies, expressive tools are a bridge towards the others. Experimenting together, we gradually build a space for taking care of ourselves and of the others. A mood of trust is established, nourished by the absence of judgement: the fact that the therapist welcomes all forms of expression, even those seemingly uncertain, absurd, or ineffective, hints to a non-judgmental attitude towards the whole person. Trust is at first catalyzed by the therapist's stance towards the group, and becomes reciprocity. Trusting both the therapist and our companions allows us to take possession of a shared space, which has a double aspect: it is safe enough to risk, and open enough to freely experiment. This trust is the sufficient condition for openness towards all that may happen; and something usually happens: we find ourselves observing amazed by many expressive abilities we did not even suspect to have.

The threefold tendency to openness, trust and wonder roused in the *exercise* manner, is the presupposition for *improvisation* as well. The expressive tools that have been experimented with are now used to create forms and figures (visual, musical, kinetic, or dramatic) in the immediacy of here and now, individually or in a group. In *improvisation, Versatility* comes into play. The expressive restraints are not given a priori: while exercise is set upon a rule, in improvisation rules are created from the process itself and can be transformed within its course. The musician Stephen Nachmanovitch reminds us, "we improvise when we move with the flow of time and with our own evolving consciousness, rather than with a preordained script or recipe" (Nachmanovitch, 1990: 17). In improvisation, any gesture, sign, word, or sound may lead to countless developments, some of which are absolutely unexpected: we deal in a practical way with flexibility. This is even more evident in group improvisation, where the presence of others is both a constraint and a resource. At the same time, we learn to cohabit with chaos: improvisations may not be coherent or congruent; they may not follow a logic development or reach a proper end; it might even happen that an improvisation collapses or gets stuck. The amount of anxiety generated by such vicissitudes is however shared and contained by the group and the therapist, and it does not overflow or compromise the process: on the contrary, it may become an energy helping it to continue. In Dramatherapy, for instance, it quite often happens that the initial embarrassment of showing oneself later becomes self-irony and the ability to laugh at oneself[27].

We can also see the elements of *Versatility* in the *composition* manner: our recovered expressive abilities have now become a shared language, which has been thoroughly explored through improvisation, and now carries a new creative experience, where an intentional design is taking shape. We have already found some qualities of *Presence* in the two manners examined above: exercise demands a focussed attention, improvisation a generalized one. Yet they manifest themselves in their clearest way in the composition manner. The distinctive signs of composition are *project* and *performance*. Project is the conceiving pattern, taking intuition as a starting point and developing it toward its completion; performance is the actual communication of the results of the project, the moment when it becomes evident. In the dynamics between project and performance, between potential and act, between future and present, intensity of experience and awareness of the present moment are interplaying, mutually empowering each other. The product of art creation is always standing in a space between the internal reality of the maker and the external reality of the living world, perceiving, and being perceived. Artists are therefore near and far from their own work at the same time. This unique perspective, which has been defined "aesthetic distance", allows us to be intensely present and quietly detached at all once, living into the fire of action yet contemplating it with no interest. (I have discussed this issue as regards to Dramatherapy under the title of "actor's paradox" in Pitruzzella, 2004). As for sense awareness, it is triggered from exercise, it has an essential function in improvisation and, in composition, it becomes an indispensable means for communication.

In Arts Therapies, therefore, the artistic process fosters and sustains creativity, being a constant training for the attitudes of which creativity is made. Yet to examine from close up the value that Arts Therapies approach may have for fostering a healthy development of individuals and removing the obstacles that block it, let us go back to our model and to what it may tell us about the role of creativity in the making of the person.

The creative position influences our way to turn towards the world, both internal (encounter with ourselves) and external (encounter with others), and to our skill in building thresholds that connect them.

To see a picture of this statement, let us try to re-examine the table of fig.1 reading it from left to right, beginning with the second line, and we will find some interesting ideas.

Openness, flexibility, and intensity of experience outline the horizon of *Relation*.

Trust, tolerance of ambiguity and aware attention outline the horizon of *Motivation*.

Wonder, humour, and sensitivity outline the horizon of *Expression*.

Relation concerns our relationship with others: meeting, listening and mirroring; constructing and maintaining affective bonds, and even closing them. The other is at the same time like me and unlike me: what is like me may fascinate or annoy me; what is unlike me may interest or frighten me. Very often, all these feelings are mixed up confusedly within us, and clarity is impossible to attain: we cannot value the meeting with others as if it were a trade. The only chance is taking a risk. Risking in relationships implies openness: that is, the ability to see in what is new a promise rather than a threat. The opposite attitude is like a

---

27   In my Dramatherapy course, students attend humour lessons, where they learn in a practical way to make a fool of themselves.

preventive war against an impending threat. Openness, to flourish, needs a readiness to grasp the other's point of view as it is, even if it is very far from ours: the inclination to conceive manifold interpretation of the world may help us to do so. The opposite is a rigid clinging to our own standpoint, along with a tendency to see what is different as wrong. Lastly, what supports the possibility itself of relationship is a focussed psychic energy: whatever its nature is, relationship stands within what Buber called "the sphere of inter-humanness" (Buber, 1925: 297), where the presence of the others renovates us and redefines us continually. What we have defined as intensity of experience, within a relationship with other human beings, engenders a sense of authenticity: on the opposite side, we have superficiality and indifference, a defence attitude, which, when predominant, can become a chronic incapacity to build and maintain relationships.

Motivation concerns our relationship with ourselves: the awareness of our own identity and of our personal resources, which we are called to manage during the journey of our lives, is a condition for giving sense to our stories. Resuming Maslow's discussion, we can distinguish a kind of motivation founded upon need and another kind founded upon the inherently human tendency of self-actualization. But I believe that these latter kinds of motivations may even exist when the primary needs (of safety, belonging, love, respect, and self-esteem) are not entirely fulfilled. It is what the great theologian Paul Tillich has called "the courage to be": "the ethical gesture through which we affirm our own being in face of those elements of our existence that are in conflict with our essential achievement" (Tillich, 1952: 8). In the creative position, we can find some helpful traces. Creative process is founded on a double act of trust: we trust novelty as bringing good, and we trust ourselves in being able to stand the encounter. The artist seeing a form will get close to it, relying on his/her own capacity to make it grow, to remodel it, and eventually to complete it. Hence, every creative experience strengthens this trust, allowing us to keep steady in time of doubt and uncertainty, to tolerate chaos and ambiguity. The sense of trust reawakened by the creative process challenges our primal insecurity of creatures with a thousand limits, which for many people becomes living daily in fear, and makes us understand thoroughly that certainty and uncertainty, safety and risk, clarity and ambiguity are two complementary faces of the same game, that we can play light-heartedly. And demands us to play it living in the moment, with eyes wide open upon the present and, ultimately, upon the simple joy of being.

Expression concerns our ability to construct and manage signals, signs and symbols (languages), which connect our internal world (our self-perception, our memory and our imagination) with the outer world (other / others, and the environment that surrounds us). This process, like the ones described above, accompanies us through our whole life: they are indeed the material which life itself is made of. From the first communications with mother to the learning of language, children move into a universe of expression, the more consistent it is, the more the others mirror it. Expressing is complying with an interior urge, and giving it a visible form in the relationship with others and with the world. The creative dimension enriches this chance with the sense of wonder, refining it with a sense of humour, and reinforcing it upon a continuous attention towards the messages of the senses. Expressing ourselves creatively is putting the world constantly into play, and inviting others to do the same.

Openness	Flexibility	Intensity	*Relation*
Trust	Tolerance	Attention	*Motivation*
Wonder	Humour	Sensitivity	*Expression*

Figure 2 The creative functions

On the specific ways in which these creative functions are reawakened and nurtured in the fields of intervention of the Arts Therapies, we will return later, in the third part. In the next chapters, we will instead have a look to the internal dynamics of the process, which can provide us with some practical ideas for activating and managing it.

Part Three

The roots of creativity

"Creative persons are capable and interested in applying their interpretative capacities and will put effort into constructing original interpretations of experience. They probably do so regularly, many times each day, but they may also bring this interpretative tendency to bear on important problems".
(Mark Runco)

"And I notice people mumble
That there are other jobs, too.
Good for you: you may carve marble,
Fight against the Asiatic flu,
Breed some oyster or some sable
Make umbrellas of a new brand
…
Me? I dig holes in the sand.

Whether you will reap the laurels
Or find chicory at hand,
May God keep you all in honour
…
Me? I dig holes in the sand".
(Ernesto Ragazzoni, *Holes in the sand*)

9. Connections

In the former two parts of this book, we started with an operational definition of creativity, founded on common sense rather than on a precise model. We went further, discovering how the signs through which it manifests itself can be read as aspects of a larger attitude of meeting the world, synthesised with the term *"person's creative function"*. We saw that it is present in any individual as a potential; that in childhood, if basic conditions are provided, it plays a fundamental role in the making of the person; and that it can be preserved in adult life as a resource. We started noticing how important cultivating or reawakening such a quality can be in education and in therapy. I hope that readers working in these fields have started to recognise some ideas for concrete applications, both as regards the ways to help our clients to improve their creative function, and as regards the ways to use our own creativity as a tool of intervention and relationship.

What we are going to begin now is an inquiry into the creative process itself, looking for those elements that rouse within us at the very moment we are creative. A glance into the soul.

To start this inquiry, we cannot avoid turning towards the narratives that in the Modern Age had replaced the cult of the soul: neurosciences and psychoanalysis. The former, on the side of *soma*. While Descartes was looking for the soul's seat in a gland, the remarkable discoveries of the neurosciences almost persuaded us to seek the mind in brain's chemistry. The latter, on the side of *psyche*. It has invited us to lean upon inner abysses we ignored so far, to fathom out the roots of our life-sickness, yet also to find unexpected aids.

Let us look at what they have to tell us about creativity.

Neurosciences

We have already discussed *arousal,* the activation of neural chains from the remote and archaic areas of the brain to the more evolved new cortex zones. It is associated with wakefulness and focused attention. This is interesting for our inquiry, as creative processes move around an alternation of tension and relaxation. The dynamics of attention expounded in Chapter 7 is a case in point. The *arousal* levels are also connected with perception processes, conditioning their hierarchy (*top-down* or *bottom-up*), as we discussed later in the same chapter. This model will turn out to be useful soon, when we will examine the steps of the creative process.

However, the most important contribution of the neurosciences to creativity inquiry must be found in the vast area of studies about the differences between the brain hemispheres. Until the Sixties of last Century, one of the two hemispheres (usually the left, controlling language) was held as dominant, while the other was considered as little more than a half-witted servant. The only way to refute this theory was to address directly the right brain, and see how it would answer. This occurred when a surgical practice was introduced to control some otherwise incurable forms of epilepsy. Cutting the *corpus callosus,* the element keeping together and connecting the two hemispheres, causes them to act as separate systems, basically autonomous, each having its own features. The American Nobel Prize scientist Roger W. Perry had the chance to study many of those brain-split subjects, and understood that the right hemisphere, although far from language, was the keeper of some essential mental features. "The right hemisphere specialities were all, of course, nonverbal, nonmathematical, and nonsequential in nature. They were largely spatial and imagistic, of the kind where a single picture or mental image is worth a thousand words". The difference between the two hemispheres' modes can be stated as follows: "the left is basically analytic and sequential, the right spatial and synthetic." (Sperry, 1981).

Beginning with these new discoveries, researchers have explored the field in many directions, emphasizing one or another feature of each hemisphere. In broad terms, the emerging picture seemed to confirm the first impressions that creativity's source is in the right brain. Some of the most common connections are listed in the following table.

Left	Right
Verbal	Non-verbal (Visual-spatial)
Digital	Analogical
Analytic	Synthetic
Reductionist	Holistic
Intellectual	Intuitive
Rational	Emotional
Convergent	Divergent
Realistic	Fantastic
Serious	Playful
Objective	Subjective
Sequential	Complex
Tending to explanation	Tending to comprehension

Figure 3: Mind qualities usually associated with the cerebral hemispheres

The two-brain metaphor was too attractive to be overlooked by common thought, and the notion of a functional difference between the two hemispheres spread widely. Eventually, it took the form of an actual "dychotomania": "a mania for splitting up all kinds of mental functions and assigning them to one of the two hemispheres" (Dacey, Lennon, 1998: 203), which ended up bringing more confusion than clarity. Yet strong is the temptation to put aside for a while any scientific decency and let ourselves plunge into a game of free association.

If we do it, we might think, for instance, of the left hemisphere as the dwelling of the male principle, and of the right hemisphere as the dwelling of the female principle. Male is reason and authority; female is intuition and comprehension. Maleness divides, femaleness contains. The male symbol is the blade; the female symbol is the chalice. Blade and chalice (swords and cups) are two of the elements of an ancient fourfold symbolism, which has been handed down until now through the playing cards, descending from the old Tarots (both a game and a fate-telling tool). According to the anthropologist Gilbert Durand, the images of the swords and the cups correspond to the two main symbolic polarities: the night and the day of the imagination. Darkness and light, clarity and mystery: the sun dispelling the clouds and revealing the world, and the twilight haze where dream and reality merge. So we might also associate left and right to time and space, the primeval couple of Chronos and Gea. Even Apollo and Dionysus, as Nietzsche envisioned them, as embodiments of order and balance the former, chaos and elation the latter. But maybe our free associations have led us too far away; it is better to close this digression (where perhaps the right brain has got the upper hand), and come back to our discourse about the brain hemispheres with a little more logic and coherence.

It has been proved that a slight activation of the right hemisphere (through hypnosis, a little amount of alcohol or psychoactive drugs like cannabis, or a specific training) can facilitate the starting of creative processes (Sternberg, 1999: 146). Nevertheless, such a start is not enough to guarantee its development, and to lead it to completion: a complete creative process is not made only of free associations and imagination, but it needs to deal with realizations and their communications to other people. Here, the collaboration of the other hemisphere is crucial.

Joseph Bogen, the neurosurgeon who collaborated with Sperry, maintains that the creative process depends on the quality of the interaction between the hemispheres. Even if there is no agreement in defining the specific functions of each of them, and probably any definition risks being restrictive, there is one point everybody agrees with: that the two brains work in different ways, and for the most part separately. In other words, in managing everyday routines, the two hemispheres often work autonomously, and "the inter-hemispheric exchange is much of the time incomplete" (Bogen, Bogen, 1999: 573). This is confirmed by the fact that "in ordinary social situations the (split-brain) patients are indistinguishable from normal in spite of the cutting of more than 200 million nerve fibres" (ibid), and they need to be specifically tested to understand the difference. What seem to be totally lacking are creative abilities. Thus, Bogen suggests taking into consideration as the source spot of creativity the *corpus callosus*, the brain area working as an interface between the hemispheres. He quotes examples of people in which a congenital atrophy or a functional damage of this brain part is connected not only with a lack of creative abilities, but also with the incapability of appreciating art works and fiction.

This seems to support our hypothesis that creativity is available to everybody (with the possible exception of the cases above mentioned), because it is engendered by an inter-hemispheric dialogue, rooted in our own brain structure. It is likely that some people have a certain easiness in such a dialogue as a congenital aptitude (and this explains why someone is more creative than others, i.e. the existence of geniuses), but, given the brain plasticity, it is possible to activate and cultivate it even for those who have never used it.

Psychoanalysis

The contribution of the various forms of psychoanalysis to creativity studies is large and manifold, especially regarding artistic creation; oddly enough, although Freud's discoveries show all the features of creative invention, scientific creativity had seldom been investigated by psychoanalysts.

The creativity notion in psychoanalysis has been developed in many different ways, which may lead to opposite views on its value in people's psychic life. We cannot follow all of them in the pages of this book. We will rather restrict our discussion to a couple of cues which may help us to understand which answers the various forms of psychoanalysis have given to the following question: where creativity comes from?

The first cue comes from Freud himself, who, in the first stage of the long evolution of his theories, relates the artist's work to sublimation. Sublimation is a non-pathological defence mechanism (unlike pathological ones, like repression, denial, and projection). It displaces a sexual or aggressive drive to a socially acceptable goal, like artistic or intellectual work. It is interesting to notice the polyvalence of the word. It is likely that Freud had chemistry in mind, where sublimation is the transition of an element from a solid to a gaseous state, skipping the passage through a liquid state. However, he could not ignore the word "sublime", meaning "what is high". Its etymology is controversial. The prefix sub- means "under"; the root could refer to "limen", which means "threshold", but also "door's architrave": in this case, what is under the architrave is high from the observer's point of view. Alternatively, it may refer to "limus" ("slanting"), so its meaning should be "what obliquely ascends". But it could be connected also with another meaning of the word "limus", that is "mud" (and this would be quite mysterious, unless we think of the Buddhist metaphor of the lotus flower, having its roots in the mud). Edmund Burke, who was a forerunner of Romantic aesthetics, discriminated "beauty" from "sublime" in the arts. Beauty is warm and reassuring; sublime is upsetting and dreadful. Beauty is tied to joy, sublime to pain.

Sublimation, for Freud, is a necessary transformation, because instinctual drives can hardly adjust to civilization, but it is nonetheless a loss, conveying a sense of resignation and discontent: only the unhappy sublimates. This aspect introduced the association of creativity with pathological states, and many scholars, following Freud's comments on Leonardo, have searched detective-like into the artists' lives, hunting for any trace of sublimated drives to be matched in their works. This has deeply influenced the arts' criticism during the XX Century, creating a new way to understand the art works. However, although it can be an interesting standpoint to clear some aspects of a single work or a single author, it does not seem to add very much to Freud's early intuition dated more than a hundred years ago, as regards the comprehension of the creative process. Nonetheless, it points out a significant remark about the force of the artistic process, connecting it with soul's motions, which are primeval and powerful. It hints to a transmutation of an ancestral energy that we share with the animals (while in them the expressions – sexual or aggressive – of such an energy are modelled from the survival instinct), into cultural forms that mark us as humans.

Still in the early Freud we find another inspiring suggestion to enter into the deep of the creative process: the conscious/unconscious dialectics. Certainly, Freud did not invent the notion of unconscious: as L.L.Whyte states, "the idea of unconscious mental processes was, in many aspects, conceivable around 1700, topical around 1800, and it became effective around 1900" (1969: 57). The unquestionable merit of Freud was that he continuously devised models accounting for this unknown part of our psyche, and its relations with the more self-aware part. In the earliest of those models, we find the distinction between primary and secondary process. These terms indicate two different ways of psychic work, one connected with the unconscious, the other with consciousness. At the roots of such a conception, there is again an idea of primordial energy, described in psychophysical terms with the drive concept, which in its manifestations at a pure psychic level is called *libido*. This psychic energy condenses around some representations, bestowing them a power upon our being persons. However, it acts in different ways in the two psychic registers, the one controlled by consciousness (largely coinciding with the Ego), and the unconscious one. At consciousness level, it can be attached to stable representations, tied with the reality principle, where the satisfaction of drives is delayed (otherwise, civilization would be impossible). Freud defined this process as secondary not to lessen its importance, but to outline that this is a most evolved psychic mode, both from ontogenetic and phylogenetic point of view. Children and savages' minds work in a different way, founded on the pleasure principle, where drives search an immediate gratification, and, if they do not find it, they fancy it.

The primary process, which in adult western people expresses itself in dreams, in dreamlike states out of the consciousness' control, and in many of the mental states classified as psychotic, utilizes, according to Freud, some curious operating devices: condensation and shifting. The former unites different elements in a unique representation; the latter replaces one element with another.

Roman Jacobson has conveyed this distinction into the linguistic field, relating condensation with metaphor and shifting with metonymy: both are basic figures of the poetic language.

In some way, the primary process challenges the foundations of reason itself, questioning two of its ground rules. The principle of identity: "everything is what it is" (Leibniz); the principle of non-contradiction: "nothing can be and not be at the same time" (Aristotle). In dreams, two people are melted into a single persona (it happens in theatre too: but it is just a fiction, for Heaven's sake!). And T.S. Eliot could see the dance "at the still point of the turning world" (*Four quartets*).

Many interesting theories of creativity have been construed upon the dialogue between primary and secondary processes. Ernst Kris, who was an art historian before being a psychoanalyst, made a passionate attempt to demonstrate that art is not just a symptom. He maintained that in art, unlike what happens in dreams and in the psychotic delirium, the Ego takes over the helm: "we are fully authorized to speak about a control of the Ego over the primary process as an extension of its functions" (Kris, 1952: 17). The artist is able to regress into the primary process, where the spring of inspiration lies. A first reworking occurs at the *pre-conscious* level, a transit station where the raw materials of the primary process prepare to show themselves to the consciousness, to become eventually art.

The Italian-American scholar Silvano Arieti, who, being a psychiatrist, was interested in ascertaining what amount of creativity was hidden in his patients' deliria, has developed this model. According to Arieti, the creative potential of the psychotic imagination is thwarted by the fact that the relation between primary and secondary process is out of balance: they do not speak to each other and often the primary process takes the upper hand. In creativity, considered by Arieti under the aspect of art, science and humour, a combination is operated instead, called *tertiary process,* in which the two are harmonized: "the tertiary process combines the two worlds of mind and matter, and, in many cases, the rational with the irrational. Instead of refusing what is primitive (or archaic, or outdated, or off the beaten track), the creative mind integrates it with normal logical processes in what appears as a 'magic' synthesis, from which the new, the unexpected and the desirable emerge" (Arieti, 1976: 13). From this formulation, the idea can derive that recovering the tertiary process, the place where different parts of the psyche entertain a positive dialogue, through the arts practice, could be a worthwhile therapeutic goal in the care of mental disorders.

Of course, there are many more contributions from psychoanalysis: among others, we must mention the remarkable theoretical statement by D.W. Winnicott, which will be taken into consideration later, discussing imagination.

Bridge-makers

For the moment, let me express my sincere admiration for the impressive analogies between two apparently inconsistent thought systems. (Even if one of the most quoted statements ascribed to Freud is that eventually biology will replace psychoanalysis, and many have seen in the discoveries about the split brain the confirmation of some psychoanalysis' basic assumptions, which have never had any scientific validation so far. To tell the truth, such a validation has never actually been searched). And allow me a final go-round with free associations evoked by those analogies.

First, I happily notice that we are probably made of two parts, each of them being important in its own way. Each of these parts makes its own reality, which can alternate, integrate, or overlap: Chuang-Tzu dreamed he was a butterfly, and when he woke up, he did not know if he was Chuang-Tzu who had dreamed to be a butterfly, or a butterfly dreaming then to be Chuang-Tzu. In the story, the two worlds overlap, suggesting how ambiguous our perception of reality may be. Yet Chuang-Tzu is also the author of the tale itself, and in the literary act (including in its parable the relationship with the reader, as any artistic gesture requires a witness) they integrate. But it is necessary to have words to tell it, and words are all on one side: on the other, there are images, sounds, movements. If they are not helped, the images will keep staying down there, and, being powerful as they are, they can come out suddenly, in a destructive way. The sleep of reason engenders monsters (but what about the unicorn and the phoenix? Are they monsters as well?). Or else, at other times, they interweave a dance of order and chaos, of light and darkness, Mythos and Logos, and then something new can happen.

Leaving aside fanciful thoughts, probably the equation left hemisphere = unconscious / right hemisphere = consciousness will not hold water, unless we take it as a metaphor. Yet this metaphor may enlighten us on a point of our inquiry into creativity: both neurosciences and psychoanalysis identify as the cradle of creativity an intermediate land between two opposite psychic spheres, separating and connecting them at the same time. Whether it is the tertiary process or the corpus callosus, creativity springs up from a bridge, and such a bridge must be guarded, reinforced, and constantly cared for.

10. Inspiration and Elaboration

The name of Graham Wallas (1858-1932) is one of the most frequently quoted in creativity studies. His four-step model, although the radical cognitive psychologists look at it with a certain suspicion, is still one of the most popular descriptions of the creative process. In addition, it is quite odd that such an influent model was neither conceived by a psychologist, nor by a scientist, nor even by an artist.

Wallas was actually a rather eclectic character, gifted with intuition and passion, who crossed through different fields with an infectious curiosity: a Victorian age intellectual, who dropped his family's Catholicism to embrace the socialist faith, and became one of the promoters of the Fabian Society. His major work, *Human Nature in Politics*, was issued in 1908, after he left the Fabians, blaming their feebleness in contrasting the English imperialist foreign politics. The book was influenced by Gustave Le Bon's *Psychology of the Crowds* (which also aroused Freud's interest), and it is an invitation to rethink politics by considering that not all the motivations of people's behaviour are governed by reason. He suggests that psychology should help politics to be restored (and it sounds strangely up-to-date...). In the last part of his life, he devoted himself to an introspective study of mental processes, and at the age of 68, he wrote *The Art of Thought*, where his model of the creative process is expounded.

Phases of the creative process

Wallas construes his model starting from a statement that the great German physicist Hermann von Helmholtz pronounced at a banquet for his seventieth birthday. The old scientist, talking about his discoveries, had explained the birth of "happy ideas", those sudden thoughts, apparently coming out of the blue, solving long brooded problems abruptly and without a deliberate effort. He asserted that they came to his mind as inspirations, not at the closure of a long research endeavour, or at the end of a day at his desk, but rather during a walk on the hills on a sunny day.

In this short account, Wallas traces the first three phases of the creative process, calling them in order: *Preparation, Incubation,* and *Illumination.*

The Preparation phase is when the conscious mind analyses a problem in all its aspect, yet not coming to a solution.

In the Incubation phase, conversely, the mind is provisionally averted from the problem; it can be either concentrated on something else, or relaxed. Other kinds of forces act in this phase, beneath consciousness.

The Illumination phase is when an answer suddenly appears, often as an image or a clue to be developed.

To these three phases, Wallas adds another one, calling it *Evaluation.* This is inspired by the words of another scientist, the French mathematician Jules-Henri Poincaré.

Poincaré told his creative experience in terms very much like Helmholtz's: his illumination, which allowed him to solve a complex mathematical riddle, occurred when he stepped on the footboard of a departing train. (The necessity of referring to unconscious factors to explain creativity had already been stated by the pioneer of French psychology, Théodule Ribot, who however warned: "Inspiration is the result of an underground work, existing in every person; in some people it is at a highest level. Being unknown the nature of such a work, nothing can be said about the ultimate nature of inspiration"[28]). Yet Poincaré is the first to mention the unconscious as an advocate of mathematics. Of course, Poincaré's unconscious is not the same as Freud's. He gives a rather self-evident definition, in that he calls "the subliminal I" (which has an etymology similar to "sublime", yet indicating "what is beneath the threshold") anything which lies under the conscious level, with no attempt to define its structure.

The main aspect of Poincaré's remarks retrieved by Wallas was its stress on the fact that the unconscious mind provides not "ready-made solutions", but that an extra work of elaboration and evaluation is required.

From these few cues, connecting them to his personal experience, Wallas creates his fascinating model. He warns, however, that it is just an attempt to single out a recognizable structure within a continuous process. Not always do the four phases present themselves with the same clarity as the above examples. The preparation phase, for instance, especially in the artistic creation, might not be focused on a specific problem. "It must always be remembered that much very important thinking, done for instance by a poet exploring his own memories, (…) resembles musical composition in that the stages leading to success are not very easily fitting into a 'problem and solution' scheme" (Wallas, 1926: 83). It might alternate many times and in various ways with moments of incubation and illumination; incubation itself can occur either when the mind is relaxed or when it is engaged in other problems, sometimes of a completely different range.

Though being more descriptive than explicative, and, all in all, leaving unsolved many aspects, Wallas' model is nonetheless challenging, and invites us to further thoughts. The first noteworthy issue is its emphasis on the irrational features of the creative process, not only in the artistic, but also in the scientific field. The other significant aspect is the fact that the relation between the elements of the process, the proportion of "inspiration and transpiration", which Edison estimated at a rate of 1 to 99%, here is about 50 to 50. Preparation and evaluation are on one side, incubation and illumination on the other.

Inspiration

It is curious enough that a strong emphasis on the importance of irrational aspects of the creation has came from the most exact among the sciences: mathematics. After Poincaré, another great French mathematician, Jacques Hadamard, lingered upon non-conscious mental procedures, claiming that their task is not only to generate ideas, but also a work of pre-selection of the best ones, worthy to be brought to consciousness. Hadamard mentions a series of mathematical intuitions whose mechanisms remained partially "unknown even to the thinker who found them" (1945: 109).[29]

---

28   Ribot, 1990: 49.
29   An outstanding example is Fermat's theorem, which was enounced with no demonstrations by the author, and had needed three centuries to be proved.

In short: Wallas' model describes a creative process developing itself along two polarities: one is under the consciousness' shield; conversely, the other works in an autonomous way, out of its control. It is just in this one (the incubation/illumination axis) that the specificity of the creative process is located, although the dialogue between the two polarities is crucial for the completion of the process. We will explore these polarities starting with the terms used by Wallas himself.

Incubation recalls Ribot's "underground work". The word derives from the Latin verb "incubare", which means "brooding": in this sense, it has been retrieved by modern medicine to indicate the first stage of an illness, when the infection spreads into the body, before symptoms appear. "Incubare" (like the Greek *en-koimaomai*, from which it derives) means also "lying" or "sleeping": it denoted the act of sleeping inside a temple. Such a tradition was tied to the cult of Asclepius (Aesculapius in Latin), the demigod presiding over care and healing. Various stories circulate about his origins: Diodorus Siculus maintains that he was the son of Apollo and a young maiden, who abandoned him on a mountain near Epidaurus, where the main temple was to be built. A shepherd found him there, and realized his divine nature seeing him shining. Asclepius was a healer, taught in the art of medicine by Chiron, the Centaur, and he reached the point of raising the dead, provoking the wrath of Zeus, who killed him[30]. In the temple of Asclepius, the believers spent the night, waiting for the god to appear in their dreams, to advise a treatment, or directly operating on the illness. The incubation of dreams opened the door to the god.[31]

On the other hand, what all the gods have always done, including the God of the Bible and our Old Man Coyote, is "blow into", which has the same meaning as "inspiring" (in Latin: "in-spiro").

Artists have always been aware of the necessity to make an opening for the "divine power that moves you" (Plato),[32] and many art works carry a clear mark of long incubations and sudden illuminations.

The composition of Rainer Maria Rilke's *Duino Elegies* is a fascinating example, worthy of a digression. In 1912, the poet was in the middle of a crisis, both artistic and personal. After the writing of the *Notebooks of Malte Laurids Brigge,* his only long novel, where he had engaged in a severe battle with his own personal story, he felt emptied, unable both to create and to love. He refused psychoanalysis, proposed by his beloved friend Lou Salomé, telling her that it would make sense only if he intended to quit poetry: "in this case, it would be possible to chase demons, who, in a bourgeois dimension, are really annoying. And if, as it is likely, also the angels will go away with them, even this fact is to be considered as a simplification, for they surely will not be utilized in a future job (which one?)" (Rilke, Salomé, 1975: 169). He spent a long winter of discontent and sterile solitude, in voluntary exile in the Caste of Duino, near Trieste. "But one day", as it is recounted by his friend Marie Turm und Taxis, "he received a bothersome business letter. As he wanted to get rid of it as soon as he could, he devoted himself to numbers and other arid matters. Outside the castle, a violent cold wind was blowing, but the sun was shining brightly, and the blue sea was sparkling, as if embroidered with silver threads. Rilke went down to the castle ramparts, which stretched out east and westwards upon the sea, jointed at the castle's foot by a narrow path. In that point,

---

30 Kérenyi, 1963.
31 Meier, 1985.
32 *Ion, 533.*

the sheer cliffs are two hundred metres high. Rilke was walking up and down, engrossed in his thoughts, because he was worried about the answer to that letter. But suddenly he stopped in the middle of his thoughts, for he had the feeling that, in the tempest din, a voice had shouted to him: "But who, if I cry, would listen to me, among the hosts of Angels?" He stopped, listening. "What is it?" he whispered, "What is coming?" He took his notebook, which was always in his pocket, and jotted down the words, adding soon other verses springing up spontaneously. Who was coming?...Now he knew: the God...He quietly went back to his room, put the notebook aside, and wrote his business letter. That night, the whole Elegy was written" (Leppmann, 1981: 293).

He continued writing until 1915, creating the four early Elegies. Then, seven years more of silence, with a war in between. Eventually, a new season as a hermit, in the Swiss castle of Muzot, and the last, intense creative flow. The rousing event was the new of the death of a young dancer, not yet twenty, whom he had know since she was a little girl. In a few days, "like a hurricane", he composed another masterwork, the *Sonnets to Orpheus,* and completed the remaining Elegies (five to ten). "Everything in me, threads, material and loom, creaked and stooped. No time to think about food. Now I recognize myself again. It was like a maiming of my soul that the Elegies were not a reality. Now they are. I am. (Rilke-Salomé, 1975: 294-5)[33].

Ancient poets invoked the Muses (daughters of Memory) to intercede with gods. In Indian art, the genesis of the creative process is largely ascribed to a sequence like this: incubation, invocation, identification, and illumination. At the beginning, the artist moves away from everyday reality, trying to pay attention to his inner nature. He lights incense to please the deities, and prays to the god Vishmakarma (patron of creativity). Then he tries to identify himself with the subject of the painting: "only after becoming the deity in his feelings can the artist paint creatively" (Maduro, 1976[34]). We may compare it with Plato's statement: "Poets are only interpreters of the gods, possessed by each god from whom any of them is taken"[35].

Modern scholars summon neither angels nor gods. The illumination described by Poincaré and Wallas has nothing to do with them. Other terms have come into use to name this kind of phenomena: the most current are intuition and insight.

Intuition and insight share the same roots: they both mean "to see within". A glance, often abrupt, inside what is facing us, and even inside ourselves.

Intuition has been regarded as a form of knowledge for thousands of years: grasping something with no thought as a mediator. For the ancient philosophers it is a divine quality; according to C.G. Jung, it is one of the basic psychic functions[36], "conveying perceptions through an unconscious way" (Jung, 1921: 466).

Insight is a term quite widespread in contemporary psychology, since W. Köhler used it to describe a sudden "reorganization of the mental field", through which we can perceive a significant shape starting from separate elements.[37] In psychotherapy, it describes the very moment when people encounter their inner parts (emotions, feelings, memories or conflicts), which is regarded as an important step of the therapeutic process.

---

33 Two years later, Rilke was to die from the same illness that had killed his young friend.

34 Quoted in: Sternberg, 1999: 342.

35 *Ion, 534.*

36 Jung's psychic functions are divided in rational (feeling and thought) and irrational (intuition and sensation). .

37 Köhler, 1929.

However, Ribot already identified the essential signs of inspiration at the beginning of the last Century: suddenness and impersonality. "It makes a sharp irruption into the consciousness, yet it presupposes a latent work, more than often very long. It is analogous to other well-known psychic states: for instance, a passion ignored, which, after a long time of incubation, reveals itself through an act; or else a sudden decision, after a seeming endless rumination. (...) Impersonality has a deeper character than the former. It reveals a power higher than the conscious individual, stranger to him, though it works for him" (Ribot, 1900: 43).

Elaboration

In the end, it can be useful to reflect for a while upon the phases that, in Wallas' model, are considered the rational side of the process: preparation and evaluation.

We saw that the phase called preparation by Wallas is, generally, more relevant to scientific than to artistic creativity. Art usually advances in a less clear-cut way, alternating it with inspiration and elaboration.

Evaluation is instead a necessity for any creative act. It allows the process to go forward: evaluating means conferring a value to what we created, even if it is not an ultimate result, but just a stage of a longer journey.

A value for the author, but also a value for other people: it can have therefore either a personal or an impersonal aspect. The shepherd improvising a melody on his pipe (or with his trombone, like Rodari's funny character) in the lonely countryside, may feel satisfied with his performance, not needing other human beings as audience[38]; people can try to express their feelings in poems, and keep them closed in a drawer (as many of us have done, especially in our youth). In any case, the author of the creative act must possess an inner locus of evaluation.

Carl Rogers has written on this topic: "Perhaps, the most fundamental condition for creativity is: the source or the place of the evaluating judgement must be internal. The product's value, for the creative person, is not determined by other people's praises or critics, but by herself. Did I create something that satisfies me? Does it express a part of me, my feeling or my thoughts, my suffering and my ecstasy? These are the only questions that really matter for creative individuals, or for any individual in the moment they are creative" (in Anderson, 1959: 103).

On the other hand, the only creativity we can speak about, whether in arts, sciences or everyday life, is the one that becomes a social act. When we look at the interpersonal aspect of the evaluation, we must consider that the criteria with which a creative process is accepted are tied to countless psychological and cultural factors, including the creative attitude of the receiver. Works of art and scientific discoveries have been evaluated in different ways in different times and contexts. And so often the two levels (personal and impersonal) speak different languages. An immense writer like Franz Kafka found it difficult to publish his works, which were appreciated by a small group of friends and admirers (and he probably did not value them enough, if he felt the need to burn them). Moreover, the inventory of artists

---

38   But I cherish a memory of a moment of rapture, when I had been listening for a long while, without him knowing, to the music played by a shepherd on his flute, accompanied by the birds whistling, some occasional sheep bleating, and the sea roaring in the background (Contrada Zingaro, Scopello, 1972).

who were regarded as great in their time, and then forgotten, is unending, as well as the list of those who were not even recognized, and attained a posthumous glory.

If we think about school, and look at the way in which a divergent expression is often considered as a mistake, we find quite a discouraging picture. Unfortunately, it is quite rare that a pupil, proudly showing the three-eyed face she has drawn, hears her teacher saying: "Well done. Did you know that Picasso painted in the same way?" It is more likely that she rebukes her (softly, we hope), taking for granted that the girl has ignored the fact that we have only two eyes in our heads. In rough behaviourist terms, we could say that creativity, to survive, needs some kind of reinforcement. An acknowledgement that may even be very slight, yet witnesses the fact that at least another person appreciates the value of the creative act.

The relationship between the personal and the interpersonal levels of the creative process will be discussed in more detail later.

Towards a dynamic model

The brief examination of the Wallas' model has allowed us to continue our inquiry into the creative process. In the last two chapters, we have seen two different ways of psychic functioning, which we could define at a more general level as the *Inspiration* and the *Elaboration* axis, alternating all along the process.

It has been demonstrated that subjects who submit themselves to creative problem-solving tests usually have a low arousal in the incubation, a sudden pitch in the illumination, and go back to a medium level in the further phases of elaboration. However, the mere laboratory tests cannot account for the many ways in which such an alternation may manifest itself in different people and in different kinds of processes: the pace and the intensity of the arousal can actually vary a lot from person to person and from situation to situation.

This matches the limit of Wallas' model that has been outlined until now, which makes it suitable to describe some specific processes, but not flexible enough to permit a further generalization.

Perhaps, the problem is that the ways in which inspiration and elaboration interact, mutually influencing each other, are not entirely describable using a linear-diachronic model. Csikszentmihalyi, who nevertheless uses Wallas' model (with a few slight alterations), warns that if it is taken too literally "it gives a severely distorted picture of the creative process", which is actually "less linear than recursive" (Csikszentmihalyi, 1996: 60). Not only is the alternation between the two modes of psychic functioning uneven and almost whimsical, and presents itself in sequences different from those described by Wallas, but it seems also that elements of the two different modes are simultaneously present.

Furthermore, although partially patronized by the huge metaphors of the two hemispheres and of the two processes, explored in the former chapter, the conceptual construct opposing rationality and irrationality, (or consciousness and unconscious), is probably unsuitable.

I believe that the creative process expresses itself through a dynamic motion among elements generated from the interaction of the inspiration and the elaboration axes. These elements, both related to each other and independent, are at the same time rational and irrational, conscious and unconscious, pertaining to the right and to the left brain. The dynamic motion connects and harmonizes contrasting elements that usually are kept apart.

In the next chapters, I will try to illustrate this statement.

Part Four

Elements of the creative process

"Now I a fourfold vision see
And a fourfold vision is given to me
Tis fourfold in my supreme delight
And three fold in soft Beulah's night
And twofold Always. May God us keep
From Single vision & Newton sleep".
(William Blake)

"I don't see much sense in that" said Rabbit.
"No," said Pooh humbly, "there isn't.
But there was *going* to be when I began it.
It's just that something happened to it on the way."
(A. A. Milne, *The House at Pooh Corner*)

11. A dynamic model

Creativity and time

We have seen how the creative process is reluctant to be described into a time frame, made of succeeding phases. Yet in time we live, and in time the human action unwinds; and time cannot be conceived but as a series of subsequent moments. In my years of frequenting dramatic arts, in their numberless forms, I felt the need to scan the flux of the dramatic process, to fix some sequences that may account for its development in time, and provide a guide for action.

Taking as a starting point the reflection of my beloved mentor, Roger Grainger, who compares drama with ritual[39], I identified three phases in the dramatic process, which I called *Foundation*, *Creation*, and *Sharing*.[40]

Foundation is the time when the possibility itself of the dramatic act is established. Rules of the game are stated and boundaries are marked; people are invited to explore the nature of the drama, building through this exploration a shared language, an expressive universe within which everybody finds the permission to reveal themselves.

Creation is the time when the nascent expression of the first stage takes shape: narrative and dramatic imagination of each single person and of the group as a whole become visible and communicable through their transformation in actions and roles, stories and characters.

Sharing is the time when the group celebrates its own journey, thinking back to its stages and sharing its contents, and legitimating it as a space of experience, before leaving it to come back to their everyday world.

We find this threefold pattern both in the whole journey of a group (which may last months or years) and in the single session (which usually lasts no more than two hours). Such a threefold configuration suggests a sense of completeness: everything has a beginning, a development, and an end. Yet at the same time it is tendentially recursive, always hinting at a new potential beginning. Its mythic form is the hero's journey,[41] whose main movements (preparation, adventure, return) figure as both the closure of a cycle, and a starting point for the following one.

The three structures of the artistic process we have described before, *training, improvisation* and *composition,* find their place in the three phases of the drama in various ways. We have a prevalence of *training* and *improvisation* in the first phase, *improvisation,* and *composition* in the second, while all threes are present in the third, where verbal language is often used too.

When dramatherapy reaches its goals, what happens is undoubtedly a double creative process, as we defined it in the first part: "a process leading, through the regeneration and the

---

39   See Grainger, 1974.
40   See Pitruzzella, 2004.
41   See Campbell, 1949.

transformation of pre-existing elements, to the production of something new and original, generating surprise both in the creator himself and in observers". This "something" concerns some aspects of the relationships of people with themselves and with the world, aspects that are transformed and regenerated, producing new awareness that may help them in life. It also concerns the drama itself as an art, in its essence of a gesture generating sense. Often the two processes coincide: the emergence of high dramatic events, of moments that are "true", though not being "real" (which I defined "states of grace"), announces a change coming. I think the other Arts Therapists can share this: when a client produces an artistically meaningful act, it is often a sign of a reached maturation, of a critical knot to face, of a sudden opening towards new possibilities; sometimes, it is a sum of all these features.

However, the phases of the dramatic process do not correspond exactly with the phases of the creative process as we have examined it so far with Wallas' model. The contrasting modalities of *inspiration* and *elaboration* coexist from the beginning, and they are displayed in different ways in the various passages of the journey, refining along the way the quality of their interactions. Every gesture is pervaded by the creative principle; every word reveals fragments of creativity. Again, we risk slipping into a tautology: it is as if we would say that every atom of the dramatic process is creative, while we define drama as a form of art, and art is the creative process par excellence. We must take the risk of breaking the vicious circle and give names to what moves when the creative process is triggered.

Maps

What happens when people cross the threshold of drama? If I think of the countless times I have witnessed this passage, I see the manifestation of a motion in two directions. People enter into contact with themselves, and enter into contact with others. The first motion is on the inspiration axis: listening to the voices of their own inner word (memories, emotions, feelings, sensations, intuitions, but also vague and fragmented perceptions); these voices become images, symbols and sounds. The other motion is on the elaboration axis: the immediate and the intentional actions, the vital energy that pushes us to experiment, and the need for accomplishment and communication. The intersection of the two axes produces four cardinal points, which we will call *inner listening* and *imagination* on one side; *spontaneity* and *productivity* on the other (see fig. 3).

Imagination is the ability to play with images (visual, auditive, bodily, and narrative images): it relates not only with fantasy, producing worlds that are alternative to everyday reality, but it is also a special way to construe such reality.

Inner listening is the attitude to pay attention to the messages coming from our internal world: getting in touch with our feelings, emotions and affects, and even with our inner guide.

Spontaneity is connected with action (thus with the body), with vital energy, immediateness and motivation. It might be intended as the ability to respond promptly and adequately to stimuli, requests, and events of our environment, or, more generally, the ability to generate free expressive acts.

Productiveness means the ability to lead the action toward a result, transforming a potentiality into a project/object visible and shareable.

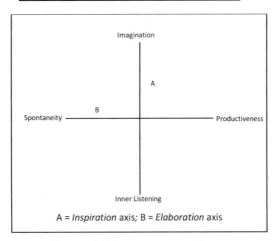

Figure 4: The intersection of axes

We may take this configuration as a first, provisional map. A map is a representation of space, useful for orientation. It is proper for human nature to divide the space into four: the space before and behind us, at our left and at our right, as if it was a projection of our own body.

In ancient cultures, such a partition was considered sacred, and it hinted to a larger correspondence between the human world and the cosmos. The four directions symbolize the cosmic order, and their centre is the Centre of the World.[42]

While three, as we mentioned before, evokes recursivity, four is the universal symbol of completeness. Not yet of perfection, because perfection is connected with the absolute form of the circle, where geometry meets the gods. The dialectics circle/square mirrors the relation between the transcendent and the immanent world, a dramatic tension toward an unreachable otherness, but yet a serene transparency of being mysteriously complementary. While the unsolvable problem of the squaring of the circle attests the impossibility to reduce infinity to finiteness, the presence of the *mandala* structure, made of concentric circles and squares, in the spiritual imagery of the whole world, signals the harmonization of the two principles on a properly human ground.

At this point, to go on with our exploration, I would like to take you for a moment to get acquainted with an image, which I consider a perfect poetic synthesis of all the discourse so far: William Blake's "fourfold vision".

Visions

Blake started from the profound belief that human nature is inherently creative: since his earliest works, he maintained that "the Poetic Genius is the True man", and he added: "All men are alike in outward form, So (and with the same infinite variety) all are alike in the Poetic Genius" (*All Religions are One*, 1788). In the works of his maturity, Blake created a powerful mythic universe, which, like the ancient myths, joins different dimensions of knowledge in a unique poetic gesture: epic-narrative, spiritual, psychological, philosophical, and historical.

---

42   See Eliade, 1964.

At the centre of the myth, we find the giant Albion, the primeval man, representing the poet himself, England and the whole humankind, including the reader. Albion is most of all the Poetic Genius, who manifests the divine nature of human beings, and in this sense, Blake compares him to Christ, who is "the Universal Man". In the poem *The Four Zoas*[43], opening the third stage of Blake's work, where the myth is wholly unfolded, he recounts the fall and the resurrection of Albion, through the separation and the eventual rejoining of his four vital principles.

The *Four Zoas* of the title are the embodiments of these principles; their names are Luvah, Urizen, Urthona, and Tharmas. Blake uses as English singular the Greek plural *Zoa* (sing. *Zoon*), which in *Apocalypse* (IV, V) indicates the four animals seen by John the Evangelist around the throne of the Lamb. They are the same animals of the prophecy of Ezekiel (I: V), wheels of God's cart. Traditionally, they are represented as a lion, an eagle, a bull, and a man, and associated with the four evangelists. Various conjectures have been made on the origin of the names. The most reliable are those connecting Luvah with *lover*, Urizen with *your reason* and Urthona with *Earth owner*. Tharmas' name is more obscure: its possible relation to the Greek word *thermos*, meaning heath, cannot be excluded[44].

In the poem, man's internal principles take their own form and identity, starting with their splitting up from their Emanation, their female counterpart. Each Zoa claims his power upon the others, and they pass from the Fall to the Apocalypse marking their reintegration, through a series of vicissitudes: separations, doublings, contrasts and collusions, escapes and abandonments, jealousies, fights and wars, chains and jails, creations and destruction of worlds, feebleness and vigour, deaths and rebirths. The four characters plainly present themselves as personifications of principles dwelling within the human soul, but they are not just symbolic abstractions: they become people too. As people, they experience the uncertainty of their identities, and they clash with their own inner divisions (the four Zoas within each of them), who engender other characters. Yet all together, they create a manifold vision opening new horizons: at the end of the poem, the Four Zoas are restored to their ancient splendour. Here are the last verses of the poem:

> "The Sun arises from his dewy bed & the fresh airs
> Play in his smiling beams giving the seed of life to grow
> And the fresh Earth beams forth ten thousand thousand springs of life
> …
> Urthona rises from the ruinous walls
> In all his ancient strength to form the armour of science
> For intellectual War. The war of swords departed now
> The dark Religions are departed & sweet Science reigns"

"Intellectual War", to which Blake had invited the reader since the beginning of the poem, is the eternal struggle of the contraries, which, in the vision of the Poetic Genius, does not

---

43 I had the chance to thoroughly study the poem while editing the first Italian unabridged edition, published in 2007 (250th anniversary of Blake's birth) by the Fondazione Piccolo di Calanovella, Capo D'Orlando-Palermo.

44 S. Foster Damon, one of the major Blake scholars, suggests that Tharmas' name may derive from "Tamas, the Hindu name for Desire" (Foster Damon, 1924: 365).

engender violence, but enlivens his world, preserving it from immobility. "Sweet Science" is the whole and integrated knowledge of the internal and external worlds, not only through the light of the intellect, but also through the body, emotions, and senses, unified by the liberating action of art.

In Blake's vision, the four principles are of equal rank, but Urthona, the Imagination, points the way to integration. For Blake, it is the supreme human faculty: "The Eternal Body of Man is The Imagination, God himself, that is the Divine Body, Jesus: we are his Members" (*Laocoon*). In addition, he maintains that it is at the root of the arts: "One Power alone makes a Poet: Imagination, The Divine Vision (*On Wordsworth*).

As we may imagine, the poem can be read at many levels, and many interpretations of its symbols have been proposed. Personally, I have met *The Four Zoas* while my study of creativity was growing, and I recognized without any doubt that these characters, with their contrapositions, fluctuations and rebalancing, were the tutelary deities of the elements of the creative process. They are autonomous, but at the same time interdependent. Each of them has his own rules and his own purpose: but rules become oppressive laws, if each of them claims his kingdom as absolute. And if, to realize his purpose, each of them needs to overcome the others, the whole system goes out of balance, and their actions end up backfiring on them. However, the harmony among the four principles is not a fixed equilibrium, but rather an incessant motion, incessantly regenerating itself.

Uthona, blacksmith and poet, is, in Blake's own words, the *Imagination*. Urizen, the reasoning faculty, ploughman and architect, patronizes *Productivity*. Tharmas, the instinctual energy, connected with the body and the senses, patronizes *Spontaneity*. Luvah, the emotion, weaver and musician, patronizes *Inner listening*. We will fond out more about them in the next chapters, when we discuss the four elements in detail.

Models

Now it is time to use our scheme, appropriately enriched, to connect visually the elements of the creative process (see fig. 5).

In the scheme, the axes of inspiration and elaboration cross each other, and each of the elements is dynamically connected with the others; the creative process is the gesture harmonizing different elements, which are complementary, contrary, or contradictory to each other.

We will return later to the meanings of these connections. Now, it would be useful to consider in depth each of the elements. This is what we will do in the next four chapters.

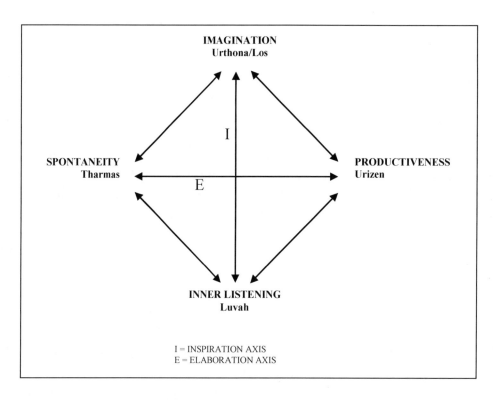

Figure 5. The elements of the creative process

12. Imagination

While the chapters on the other three elements will be more synthetic, we will linger upon imagination for longer, since it is at the very root of creativity. Among the elements we have identified, this is the one that crosses all the others, being the substance that joins them together. For many scholars, it is *tout court* synonymous with creativity: T. Ribot, the already mentioned author of the first psychological study of creativity, wrote: "creative imagination tends to manifest and to affirm itself in a work existing not only for the creator, but for the whole word" (Ribot, 1900: 8).

Following its traces, we will visit various places, and tell various stories: from myth to philosophy, from arts to science, every time the human spirit has dared to reflect on itself, the discourse on imagination has been present, being both object and subject of those reflections.

On the one hand, it preserves the continuity of existence. We close our eyes, and the world vanishes: what does make us sure that it still exists, if not our imagination? On the other hand, it is the womb of possibilities: of what is not yet, and of what might be. But also of what is not and never will be: in this sense, it is the root of falsehood and chimeras. We will see how its ambivalence is also its force, and how it has been judged differently throughout history: now as a key function of our being in the world, now as a treacherous deception and self-deception. And we might grasp why "the journey in the far off worlds of imagination may guide a dynamic psyche only along a path in the land of infinity" (Bachelard, 1943: 49).

Urthona

We will take again Blake as a starting point for this journey. Urthona is the Zoa of imagination. His name, as said before, could derive from *Earth Owner*. With this etymology, Blake seems to be suggesting a deep and unusual connection between imagination and matter. Here the first argument of Blake's theory of imagination: that fundamentally there is no difference between spirit and matter, and this oneness can be perceived through the eye of the imagination.

Yet another possible etymology is *The Fourth One*, referring to the fourth man seen by the king Nebuchadnezzar in the fiery furnace: "Did not we cast three men bound into the midst of the fire? They answered and said unto the king, True, O king. He answered and said, Lo, I see four men loose, walking in the midst of the fire, and they have no hurt; and the form of the fourth is like the Son of God" (Daniel, 3:24-5). Blake sees that 'fourth man' as a presage of Christ. This is the second argument: imagination is the divine nature in everyone.

Blake's Zoas live in a universe within the human mind, but humankind itself is contained in this universe. Like in a Möbius strip, inside and outside, though appearing different, are a single thing. Their existence develops along four levels of being, which are both manifestations of time, worlds cyclically following one another, and eternally present, because "Eternity is in love with the productions of time" (*Proverbs of Hell*). They are: *Ulro*, the material world; *Generation*, the world of vital energy; *Beulah*, the world of the soul; *Eden*, the world of the spirit. In eternity, Urthona is one and undivided; in time, he manifests himself through three characters. The first is Los, embodying the poetic art. His name could be the reverse of the word *Sol* (sun), referring to Paracelsus (we will meet him again later), considered by Blake as a master: for him, "imagination is the sun of man". Los' emanation (the female principle) is Enitharmon, whose name might derive from the Greek word *anarithmon*, meaning countless or immense; she is the incarnation of inspiration. It is worth noting that, according to Blake, the patrons of inspiration are not the Muses, daughters of Memory, but the *Daughters of Beulah*, who inhabit the city of soul. The third character is the Spectre, embodying the *techné*, the concrete capacity of realization (we must remember that Urthona-Los is also a blacksmith, and Blake himself was a skilled artisan). The Spectre is boisterous and menacing; nonetheless his presence is crucial to the poet's work, which otherwise would be no more than a solipsistic stammering.

We will entertain further considerations on Blake's doctrine of imagination later. For now, we will just outline some ideas, which will address the following inquiry.

First: imagination is the supreme creative faculty, which humans share with God: "indeed, here the two become indistinguishable," writes S. Foster Damon, (1988: 195). This faculty is expressed in art, which is analogue to God's creation. Here we find again the theme of the rivalry between man and God that we have already encountered in chapter 1, and we will meet again in the discourse on imagination, not only as a conflictive issue in the religious thinking, but also as an unavoidable metaphoric point of reference in any kind of discussion.

Blake's second significant insight is the principle that imagination expresses itself not only in the arts, but also in the world of relationship, connected with the sense of being into the sphere of inter-humanness. This is synthesized in the identification of human imagination with the figure of Christ, who, for Blake, besides being the incarnation of the "Human Form Divine", is above all the symbol of human brotherhood, born from the recognition of the spiritual nature of the other person, and from the mutual forgiveness of sins. Indeed, acknowledging the importance of human forgiveness, apart from God's justice, is the most original aspect of the preaching of Jesus Christ as reported in the Gospels, standing out against the underlying Biblical tradition (and, Blake would have added, against the way it has been manipulated later by the Earthly Church). "Mutual forgiveness of each vice / Such are the Gates of Paradise" (*For the sexes: The Gates of Paradise*).

Imagine all the people...

"Imagine there's no heaven / It's easy if you try / No hell below us / Above us only sky / Imagine all the people / Living for today..." (John Lennon, *Imagine*).

Since its beginning, humankind has had to deal with the mystery of death. Especially in the West, where the myth of the transmigration of souls has not been too successful (except for Pythagoras, who, as it is told, came across it in one of his mysterious travels to the East), the places of the otherworld have always been the imaginative answers to the anguish about our fate when our life comes to an end. The great monotheistic religions used them to establish an ethic based on reward and punishment, which often became a blackmail-like form of control over the believer's soul. Nevertheless, at the same time, they kindled the imagination of countless visionaries, poets, and artists. In the Christian cultural area, where the aversion to images was loosened earlier than in the other monotheistic religions, we have wonderful portraits of angels and devils, both in words and in images. Dante and Milton, and all the interpretations of their verses made by any kind of artists are admirable examples; Blake himself produced many remarkable pictures of *Paradise Lost*, and devoted to the *Divine Comedy* the work of his last years.

We know for certain that Purgatory, among the three realms where the soul has been imagined to go after death, is the most recent one. It was cunningly invented in the Middle Age to solve problems of power management from the Roman Church rather than for theological necessity. And we know that lately the Catholic authorities have abolished with a stroke of the pen "Limbo", the place in Hell where the unchristened souls go, which for Dante was quite a cosy spot, if compared to the torments of the rest of Hell. "We came unto a noble castle's foot, / Seven times encompassed with lofty walls, / Defended round by a fair rivulet" (IV, 106, 11). There, "into a meadow of fresh verdure" one can walk along, pleasantly conversing with noble spirits of the past: poets, scientists, and philosophers from Rome and Greece, like Ovidius, Plato and Heraclitus, and even wise men of Islam, like Avicenna and Averroes.

John Lennon, in the song that has become a sort of pacifist hymn, goes still further. He openly invites us to do without those fancies of imagination, engendered by fear and desire, which enslave us. What will come out of such a renunciation, he tells us, will be humankind living for the moment, and peacefully: "Nothing to kill or die for / And no religion too / Imagine all the people / Living life in peace". Yet the intriguing paradox breathing through the song lines is the whish that the rejection of illusion occurs through an imaginative act: what imagination creates, by the imagination can be destroyed …

Here, the power of imagination is in question: its capacity to see and make up worlds, to transform them, and even to destroy them.

After this short interlude amidst pop music and paradise, we may resume our journey in the world of imagination, and cast a glance at the ways this power (expressing, according to Blake's arguments, its godlike quality) has been portrayed in ancient times.

Adam and Prometheus

In the *Book of Genesis*, the birth of human imagination is portrayed in the challenge between man and God, causing the expulsion from the Garden of Eden, and the fall of humankind in a world of labour, sorrow, and death. It is the punishment of a jealous God for his defiant creature, who has tried to become like him. After cursing Eve, Adam and the Serpent, God said: "Behold, the man is become as one of us, to know good and evil: and now, lest he put forth his hand, and take also of the tree of life, and eat, and live for ever: Therefore the LORD God sent him forth from the garden of Eden, to till the ground from whence he was taken. So he drove out the man; and he placed Cherubims at the east of the garden of Eden, and a flaming sword which turned every way, to keep the way of the tree of life" (*Genesis*, III, 20-24).

The Hebraic term to define imagination is yetzer, deriving from the same root as *yetzirah*, creation, *yotzer*, creator, and *yatzar,* to create. The imaginative faculty owned by human beings is what allows them to cross the borders that keep them separate from God, in a repetition of the original creative act.

Doing this, they acknowledge the existence of good and evil. Erich Fromm has written: "The word *yetzer* derives from the root YZR, 'shaping', and 'moulding' (like the potter moulds a clay vase). *Yetzer* means 'form', 'structure' and 'purpose'. So the word *yetzer* means also 'images' (good and bad)...The significant point is that the Hebraic word indicates that the good and bad impulses are possible only on the base of what is specifically human: the imagination" (Fromm, 1966: 108-9).

There is an interesting analogy with the Latin verb *fingo* (whence the word "fiction" derives), which "refers in its primary meaning to the art of the potter and the sculptor, who give form to raw material with their own hands: *to form, to shape, to mould, to carve* (bringing to mind the biblical God who created man from dust). In a figurative sense it means (besides *to pretend, to simulate) to make, to create,* and also *to form, to educate, to instruct,* and finally *to imagine, to fancy, to suppose*" (Pitruzzella, 2004: 51).

In Fromm's radical reading, imagination is the utmost creative potentiality: it is comparable to God's power to create, but on a fully human plane. Such a claiming of imagination as a deeply human quality is actually a modern notion, as we will see later.

In the Bible tradition, since its first appearance the human imagination is presented as wretched, as it may mean a reiteration of the primeval transgression and a new challenge to God: therefore, it has to be discouraged. Furthermore, imagination creates false idols, like the Golden Calf, knocked down by Moses to establish the stone-written law, which was committed to him by a God who (imaginatively) manifested himself in a flaming bramble bush. Hence, maybe, the prohibition, remaining in the Hebrew culture until modern times, of representing with images anything pertaining to divinity. (However, I could see how the need to make images might have persuaded some to contrive cunning stratagems: what appeared as a "halftone screen" graphic representation of the head of Moses himself was actually made of minuscule letters forming the text of a prayer).

The tension between divine and human creation is portrayed in the *Golem* legend, widespread all over the world by the Diaspora, which has powerfully influenced modern imagery, producing countless variations, from the human *bricolage* of Mary Shelley's monster, to the disturbing genetic engineering of Aldous Huxley's *Brave New World*.

This is the story as usually told: after many years of studies and experiments in the seclusion of his dusty laboratory, a wise rabbi succeeds in creating a living being, to use it as a servant for tiring jobs. He moulds it in clay and insufflates part of his own life spirits into it. But the creature is strange and upsetting: as it passes, the rabbi's cat hides. Eventually, the Golem slips out of his control, becoming more and more dangerous and ravaging the whole ghetto. At the end of the story, the rabbi is forced against his will to kill it. Deprived of its vital energy, the Golem collapses and becomes dust – which is exactly the punishment to which the rebel Adam was condemned by God: to "return unto the ground; for out of it wast thou taken: for dust thou art, and unto dust shalt thou return" (*Genesis*, III, 14-19).

The Golem legend is a further warning against the ambition of man to rise up as a creator, letting his imagination go astray, removed from the rules established by God: this is the evil imagination, *yetser hara*. But if imagination also concerns the good, then another form of imagination is indeed possible and desirable: as the philosophy historian Richard Kearney writes, while *yetser hara* "epitomizes the error of history as a monologue of man with himself, the good imagination (*yetser hatov*) opens up history to an I-Thou dialogue between man and his Creator. This is no doubt why the Talmud declares that "god created man with two *yetsers*, the good and the evil" (Kearney, 1988: 47).

In Judaism, imagination is connected with the ethical distinction between good and evil; it implies a risk, being of the same nature as the transgressive act through which Adam challenged God, but it is in itself redeemable if submitted to the acceptance of human destiny, therefore in harmony with the utmost will. However, the analogy itself between human and divine imagination highlights a basic feature, reaching even modern creativity inquirers like us, who may state it as follows: imagination affects reality. We will see later how this idea manifested itself in modern times. For now, let us follow some traces about the ways imagination has been conceived in another culture also standing at the roots of Western thought.

If Adam is condemned to worldly existence, "in sorrow shalt thou eat of it all the days of thy life; Thorns also and thistles shall it bring forth to thee" (*Genesis*, III, 14-19), Prometheus has no better fate.

His name suggests his nature: Prometheus means "foreseer", and looking into the future is an imaginative act indeed. He was one of the Titans who went over to the enemy (the Gods), but he probably remained a rebel in his hearth. First, he created humankind, moulding it (once more) in clay; for many of the Gods, Zeus included, it was quite a nuisance. Prometheus' transgression went further: he stole fire from the Gods, practically under Zeus' nose, giving it to humans. It is also told that he gave them techniques and arts. Zeus, as usual, lost his tempers (there were very few Gods not suffering from fits of anger!), and condemned him to a rather unpleasant punishment: he was enchained, naked, in the snow of the Caucasian peaks, tormented by an enormous bird of prey (an eagle, or a vulture), feeding itself with his liver, which every night was growing anew. There he stood for thirty, or a thousand, or thirty thousand years, until the valiant Hercules, back from one of his labours, freed him, killing the insatiable bird with an arrow.

The liver detail is quite interesting. It is the only body organ able to regenerate itself (and the Greeks probably knew it): in this sense, we may glimpse a first symbolic connection with imagination. We can envisage a more profound nexus if we think that the liver has always been related to the art of divination. For the ancient foretellers, the liver of the sacrificial animals was a tool of great value, to be read like a text revealing prophecies. We have some remarkable archaeological finds from faraway cultures suggesting its importance. One is an Etruscan bronze liver, engraved with some mysterious markings (organized in multiples of four), probably hinting at a cosmic order; the other is a terracotta one, from the Sumer civilization. Both the objects were probably used for rituals of foretelling. And I have heard recently that if you go into the Battiferro cave (in the countryside of Rome), and if you eat a raw donkey liver there, you will incubate a dream revealing who you really are.

Back to Greece, even Plato ascribed to the liver, generally considered the lowliest of the body organs, the function of abode of the imagination. It has been put by the Gods in its place, guarding the organs that are farthest from the head, the body part where the immortal principle resides. Stomach and genitalia are indeed the dwellings of the lower appetites, tied there by the Gods, "just like a fierce beast, that, being inseparable from us, we are forced to feed, if the mortal kind should endure" (*Timaeus*, 71). These parts do not "listen to reason": they cannot be easily submitted by the force of thought, and are inclining to be "seduced by images and appearances". However, the liver protects them: being created shiny like a mirror, it reflects back those images, flavouring them with its bitterness, to frighten them and prevent them from running wild. Yet sometimes an uttermost inspiration "gladdens and cheers up the part of the soul that inhabits the liver", and manifests itself as prophetic imagination, in dreams or in special states of consciousness, due to "illness or some divine madness".

It is worth noting that here Plato shows a certain respect for imagination: it needs indeed to be controlled and checked by the intellect, which can discern prophecy from illusion and interprets "enigmatic voices and visions"; nonetheless, if inspired by higher powers, it can sustain a divinatory form of knowledge, able to pursue the truth.

Elsewhere, the philosopher displays a positive contempt towards imagination, based upon an idea that will remain in charge for almost the next two thousand years as the only key to understanding imagination: the idea that it is essentially a reproducing function. Meanwhile, the notion of a creative imagination will disappear under the surface in Western thought, at least until the Renaissance.

The myth of the Cave, included in the *Republic*, one of the most famous dialogues, with his dismal picture of a chained mankind, taking as real the shadows on the walls, hints to a suspicion toward images. This suspicion will later become (X, I-VIII), a straight refusal. Plato tells us that things of the visible world are nothing but imitations of the ultimate principles dwelling in the spiritual world, which may be grasped only by a purified intellect. Thus, as art can only make copies of the world, it stands at three degrees of distance from truth. A bed is taken as an example: there is the essence of the bed in God's mind; the actual bed, made by the craftsman, and the painted bed of the poor artist, who had to take the artefact as his model. Painted images are therefore only imitations of imitations, mimicries of mimicries, treacheries keeping us far from truth. In the ideal society, they need to be limited and controlled. (I wonder how much truth Plato would find in Van Gogh's *Bedroom*).

Plato's condemnation of art must be put into the wider framework of the key question enlivening his thought, and generally marking the birth of Western philosophy: the question of the ultimate knowledge. Philosophers intended to leave apart myth, which had been the sole form of knowledge in humankind's childhood. Therefore, myth is debased as illusory storytelling, good at least as a parable to illustrate an argument, but fatally deceitful in its deep matter. The *Mythos* goes behind to give room to the *Logos*, the power of the intellect, the unique power able to reach Truth (*Aletheia*) and Knowledge (*Episteme*). Imagination, in its magnificent ambiguity, cannot but be placed in the realm of opinion (*Doxa*), which is inconsistent, polemic and elusive, and is to be considered the mother of delusion and mistake.

Notwithstanding the indirect rehabilitation done by Aristotle, who gives a social value to tragedy (which is, after all, nothing but a work of *mimesis*, imitation), nobody will talk anymore about imagination for quite a while, at least in the Western world. In Mediaeval Europe, where the dominant culture was sternly influenced by the alliance between religion and philosophy, the few recorded hints are intended to reproach it as a hoax, like in Saint Augustine, or to reconsider it as a sort of maidservant of memory, like in Thomas Aquinas.

Not so in the Muslim world, where a powerful theory of imagination has been developed, too complex to give a thorough account of it here. We will just try to sketch it roughly. According to Henri Corbin, in Western thought tormented by the dualism of perception and intellect, it was not possible to find a proper place for imagination as a form of understanding.

It could be considered exclusively as the producer of imagery, namely "of the unreal, of the mythical, of the fiction" (Corbin, 1979: 15). In the Islamic philosophy of the Middle Ages, conversely, imagination is appraised as a means of knowledge. What does it know? The answer to this question is to be found in the doctrine of the three worlds: the world of pure essences (*'ālam 'aqlī*), which can be grasped by the intellect; the tangible world (*'ālam hissī*), which we perceive through the senses; and between them lies the *mundus imaginalis* (*'ālam mithālī*), the world of the soul, where angels dwell. The dynamic imagination within us permits us to approach such a world. "It is a power essentially medial and mediator, just like the universe to which it is subordinated (...) is a universe essentially medial and mediator, an intra-world between what can be sensed and what can be learned through the intellect, without which the articulation of sense and intellect would be blocked" (ibid).

Oddly enough, in spite of the silence of the philosophers, the Middle Ages were the richest season for imagination that the whole of Europe remembers. It is enough thinking that the majority of the fairy tales that grannies have told for centuries, until recent times, have their roots then. Rich in marvels is the medieval lore, as are the fairy tales that derived from it, passing through a whirlwind of countless influences (Islamic, Celtic, Oriental, and Classic). The folk sense of wonder springs up constantly in them, telling of a world where magic peeps out from every door ajar, and where a weak little man gifted with sufficient imagination can easily overcome a giant.

The arts historian Jurgis Baltrušaitis revealed how a great part of the arts and crafts of the time was marked by a bursting fantasy, welcoming and synthesizing all kinds of influences, from Celtic monsters to Chinese dragons. An imaginative wealth, which found its climax and its swan song in the visions of Hyeronymus Bosch[45].

The spark and the lamp

The greatest among the humanists, Michel de Montaigne (1533-1592), could not conceal his astonishment before the quasi-magic efficacy of imagination:

"Some attribute the scars of King Dagobert and of St. Francis to the force of imagination. It is said, that by it bodies will sometimes be removed from their places; and Celsus tells us of a priest whose soul would be ravished into such an ecstasy that the body would, for a long time, remain without sense or respiration. St. Augustine makes mention of another, who, upon the hearing of any lamentable or doleful cries, would presently fall into a swoon, and be so far out of himself, that it was in vain to call, bawl in his ears, pinch or burn him, till he voluntarily came to himself; and then he would say, that he had heard voices as it were afar off, and not did feel when they pinched and burned him; and, to prove that this was no obstinate dissimulation in defiance of his sense of feeling, it was manifest, that all the while he had neither pulse nor breathing" (*Essais*, I, 21).

What meaning does the philosopher assign to this series of very dissimilar wonders (stigmata, levitation, trance), to which he adds other strange episodes when imagination plays nasty tricks, like growing horns on a king's forehead, or a penis on a young maid? First, he seems to show an ironic detachment: "It is very probable, that visions, enchantments, and all extraordinary effects of that nature, derive their credit principally from the power of

---

45   See Baltrušaitis, 1972.

imagination, working and making its greatest impression upon vulgar and more easy souls, whose belief is so strangely imposed upon, as to think they see what they do not see" (ibid). It is worth noting that Montaigne does not question straightforwardly the actual truth of the events, but he limits himself to ascribing their cause to a naïve imagination storming over unprepared minds.

Yet later, in the same chapter, he devotes a long passage to explain imagination's effectiveness in healing, taking as example people to whom "just the sight of the medicine produced the desired effect" and some illness generated by the imagination, and healed by the imagination itself. The idea that imagination affects healing is paired with the idea that imagination creates the illness: "Now all this may be attributed to the close affinity and relation betwixt the soul and the body intercommunicating their fortunes" (ibid).

Only recently modern medicine has started, although slowly and awkwardly, to rediscover this simple idea, which was taken for granted by the solitary thinker of the XVI Century. Such an idea had been at the core of the practice of a singular magician and alchemist, a little preceding Montaigne, who was actually the first modern physician: Teophrastus Bombastus von Honenheim called Paracelsus (1493-1541). He revolutionized the paradigms of medicine in his time, which were founded upon a dogmatic reading of the classic tradition (especially Latin and Greek), opening the doors to empiricism: according to him, the physician must learn things "from nature; not from authority, but from his own experience".

Carl Gustav Jung studied thoroughly the works of the wizard-doctor who was his compatriot, and he maintained that "Paracelsus appears to be a pioneer not only of the chemical medicine, but also of empiric psychology and of psychological therapy" (1941: 226). Remedies come from nature, by virtue of the correspondence microcosm – macrocosm, standing at the roots of magic and alchemy. Nonetheless, healing is not only the effect of medicines, but is mainly tied to imagination, which is the messenger between the two realms: it represents the wholeness of man containing the universe containing man. Paracelsus' imaginative healing acted through words, arousing the subject to a symbolic journey within his own illness, and accompanying him to a concrete solution. Human imagination is the main healing factor. For Paracelsus, it is *lumen naturae*, nature's light, different from the supreme light, which people seldom see, projecting shadows onto the world, like the flames out of Plato's cave. Nevertheless, under the shadows a spark is lighted: if it is nurtured, it manifests itself in all its splendour, revealing the intimate correspondence between "the external and the internal heavens".

This is the imaginative thread running through the passage from Middle Ages to Modernity, clearly present in some cultural trends like magic and alchemy, which found their peak synthesis in the Renaissance, and have been condemned by the Church and scorned by Science. What survived the persecutions debased itself in witchcraft, and in rough chemistry. However, the importance and the qualities of Renaissance magic and alchemy have lately been rediscovered, all through the last century.

The correspondence microcosm – macrocosm is synthesized in a quite compelling way in the magic-spiritual practice called mnemonics. It was embodied, almost proverbially, by the noble savant Giovanni Pico della Mirandola (born in 1563; died in his thirties, probably poisoned); practiced, among others, by Giordano Bruno, (born in 1548; death at fifty-two on a stake), the rebel monk who was going to be remembered as a martyr of free thought. Mnemonics was born, in ancient Greece, as a practical method to remember. For example, a palace was imaginatively built, with many rooms for storing in an orderly way the elements to memorize. The place where memories can be stored might also be a visualization of the Zodiac, or a theatre, or anything else. In the XV and XVI Centuries, it was developed and established as a training of the mind to make up imaginative structures fit to contain some "fundamental and archetypical images, presupposing, as a mnemonic localization system, the cosmic order itself, so allowing a deep knowledge of the universe" (Yates, 1969: 213). Through those symbolic elements, the magician rebuilt the world within himself, not only in order to know it, but also to act upon it, by the virtue of the law of *sympathy*, expressing the intimate universal harmony. "The magician does not break the natural order, but rather he subdues it to his will, accomplishing and arranging the energies that lie scattered and dispersed all around nature" (Abbagnano, 1979, II: 75).

The *vis imaginationis* flourishes as a mediator and as a messenger between the levels of being (the worlds mirroring each other); therefore, it is the first and the uppermost among the human faculties, because it allows us to penetrate the secret consonances ruling the universe, and discern our place within it. The magician, who controls nature attuning himself to it, is the model of man who lives in harmony with the universe. So Pico puts forward "regenerative peace" as the ultimate goal of wisdom: "the invoked peace, the holy peace, the indissoluble bond, the consonant friendship, for which all men not only get in tune with the unique mind over every mind, but in an ineffable way they all merge into one" (*Oratio de hominis* dignitate, 1486, in Abbagnano, 1979: 73).

On a more concrete psychological level, it was already maintained by Aristotle that imagination connects the cognitive faculties peculiar to every human being, namely sensation and intellect; furthermore, it is their common source. According to Frances Yates, Giordano Bruno considered imagination as "the spring of psychic energy" not only as regards our experience of the world, but also our relationship with it: it is "the door leading to all the intimate affections, and the bond of bonds" (*De Magia*, in Yates, 1964: 291). This reminds us of Blake's notion of imagination as relationship, which will be considered again later.

Finally, we could hazard to say that placing imagination within the human territories, as the Renaissance magicians did, is conforming to the rising mythology of the individual as protagonist of his fate and as a force generating history, which is at the very roots of Modernity (embodied also by the sceptic Montaigne).

Here we start glimpsing a new notion of imagination, qualitatively different from the classic ones, which can be synthesized in Paracelsus' vision: the "sparkle in the darkness" which is "the sun of man". We see two new arguments emerging.

Firstly, as we have seen, imagination is positively removed from the vicelike grip of its rivalry with God, and put into the soul as a proper human feature, witness to the basic harmony between humans and nature.

Secondly, the reproducing function of imagination is not denied, but it is considered secondary to the creative function: the servant bringing materials to the maker.

We will return to these issues later. Now, let us linger a moment upon the ways this notion has been reworked inside the cultural movement that, two centuries later, fervidly reintroduced the value of imagination: Romanticism.

The clearest and the most concise description of the romantic theory of imagination is to be found in a brief passage of the rich and tangled *Biographia Literaria*, by the English poet Samuel Taylor Coleridge (1772-1843). It is worth quoting it at length.

"The Imagination then I consider either as primary, or secondary. The primary Imagination I hold to be the living power and prime agent of all human perception, and as a repetition in the finite mind of the eternal act of creation in the infinite I AM. The secondary Imagination I consider as an echo of the former, co-existing with the conscious will, yet still as identical with the primary in the kind of its agency, and differing only in degree, and in the mode of its operation. It dissolves, diffuses, and dissipates, in order to recreate: or where this process is rendered impossible, yet still at all events it struggles to idealize and to unify. It is essentially vital, even as all objects (as objects) are essentially fixed and dead. FANCY, on the contrary, has no other counters to play with, but fixities and definites. The fancy is indeed no other than a mode of memory emancipated from the order of time and space; while it is blended with, and modified by that empirical phenomenon of the will, which we express by the word Choice. But equally with the ordinary memory the Fancy must receive all its materials ready made from the law of association" (Coleridge, 1817: 233-4).

Ever since the times of Paracelsus, a clear distinction was made between *Phantasia (Phantasey)* and *Imagination*, whereas the two terms had been previously used as synonyms. Jung tells us that in the alchemy treatises of early XVII Century, *phantasia* "was indicating a subjective invention, playful, with no objective truth", while *imagination* meant "an imaginative and creative activity of the human mind" (Jung, 1942: 205). The Greek term *phantasia*, which meant also "performance" and "vision", derives from the verb *phainomai*, "to appear, to show oneself, to manifest oneself"; it is related to words like "epiphany", real apparition, and "phantom", illusory apparition. The Latin *imagination* is connected instead with the word *imago*, of uncertain etymology, which means, besides "image, figure", also "portrait" and, once more, "phantom, ghost". As often happens in these reckless etymological rebounds, we discover a curious note: both the words, in their origins, have something to do with both the arts and the supernatural. Blake, as we said before, was deeply influenced by Paracelsus, and he compared *phantasy* to *fancy*, while he saved the term *Imagination* for the creative principle embodied by Los-Urthona. The ascription of different meanings to the two words is therefore almost arbitrary, but it underlines the necessity to discriminate between two different faculties.

Coleridge calls *fantasy* the mere capacity of the mind to evoke absent objects: basically, a kind of memory. Perhaps it is a little more shifting and elusive than the sheer visual memory; a little more reluctant to be controlled by the consciousness than the encoded memory by which we learn Latin and mathematics. Yet it obeys the same rules, namely, according to the poet, the laws of association (classically: contiguity and similarity).

The discourse on imagination is far more complex. First, it is as if Coleridge retrieves the Hebraic notion of *yetzer* under the light of a non-theistic spirituality (which can do without the idea of a God-father). In other words, primary imagination is the creative energy moving an intelligent universe, manifesting itself within us as a potential state in the very moment we exist. However, this energy cannot but turn towards the finitude of the human world, with all its limits, its impossibilities, its borders. Humanizing itself, imagination, although still maintaining its primary nature, finds suitable ways to express itself in the finite world: this is art. The artist manipulates images (provided by the *fantasy*), but its work is not a mechanical rearranging or recombining, according to more or less established aesthetic laws. It is rather the creation of a new life, which, to realize itself, may even need to destroy the images from which it has been generated.

Such secondary imagination, whose accomplishment is the artistic vision, although being only "an echo of the first", allows us to perceive the thin threads connecting human beings with the soul of the universe. Charles Baudelaire, with a clear provocative intent, wrote that "imagination is the most scientific among human faculties, because it alone intuits the universal analogy, what mystic religions call *correspondence*" (Letter to A. Toussenel, 1856). And he dedicated his famous poem to these correspondences:

> "Nature is a temple where living pillars
> Sometimes give voice to confused words;
> Man passes through forests of symbols
> Observing him with familiar eyes"
> (*Correspondences*)

In the verses, the image of the forest, an element of the natural world, overlaps with the image of the temple, the sacred space, built by humans to welcome the gods. The ancient language of gods is too far from our capacity of understanding, a horizon so unreachable to appear insubstantial, like the rainbow's end. Yet imagination is able to see the symbols lying in every thing. Symbols are unintelligible, as they are referring to something else that reason alone cannot grasp. As imagination resounds with the innermost texture of reality, it can open the way to a comprehension of symbols. Only if we are willing to be observed by them.

Letting ourselves be observed by the symbols is not simple passivity; yet it is an attitude of active reception, an opening towards the mystery affecting us even before we know it. It is giving permission to our whole self to vibrate in unison with symbols, which does not mean an annihilation of the self, nor yet being seized by the power of symbols, in an unspeakable mystic union, but rather a preliminary condition allowing us to assimilate them, and return them to our fellows through the poetical creation. According to Percy Bysshe Shelley, each of us is like an Aeolian lyre, exposed to "the alternations of an ever-changing wind, which move it by their motion to ever-changing melody. But there is a principle within the human being, and perhaps within all sentient beings, which acts otherwise than in the lyre, and produces not melody alone, but harmony, by an internal adjustment of the sounds or motions thus excited to the impressions which excite them" (*Defence of Poetry*, 1821).

Blake's view was after all not so dissimilar from Coleridge and the other Romantics. With the difference that Blake was not fearful to call traditional religious symbols into the arena, reinventing them under the light of his own vision: for him, the "great task" of the poet is

> "To open the Eternal Worlds, to open the immortal Eyes
> Of Man inwards into the Worlds of Thought: into Eternity
> Ever expanding in the Bosom of God, the Human Imagination"
> (*Jerusalem*, 5: 18-20)

To conclude, we have seen the two conflicting notions of imagination in antiquity: creative imagination, usurped by man to God, and mimetic imagination, which can only reproduce things: the Hebraic *yetzer* and the Greek *phantasia*. In Modern Age, the two opposites are transcended into a synthesis, rooting it into the individuals as a function that allows them to go ahead of themselves, towards a connection with the spiritual principle that we share with all the living beings ("For everything that lives is holy", as Blake used to say).

In the Renaissance magic-alchemic idea, it is the source of magic, the human ability to influence the rhythms of the cosmos, attuning oneself to them and penetrating their secrets.

In the Romantic aesthetic-cognitive idea, it is the root of poetry, and of all the arts, rejecting imitation and being restored as invocation and evocation.

Symbols

In this synthesis, imagination is regarded as a form of knowledge, because it appears to be, as Baudelaire realized, of the same nature of the symbols. A symbol is an image that at the same time conceals and unveils a profound sense, going beyond the literal meaning, and heralding a mystery. It is neither a signal nor an allegory; it is neither readable in terms of a clear correlation between signifier and signified, nor entirely explainable in words.

Most of the spiritual knowledge of humankind is expressed in symbols. The paradox of the deepest and darkest parts of our souls coinciding with the brightest, the unspeakable epiphanies of the ultimate sense of things, the utmost synthesis of the irretrievable conflict between life and death, freedom and fate, futility and worth of human efforts: we find all this in countless symbolic narratives, from the oldest creation myths to the mystic vision of Ste Hildegard, from the journeys of Gilgamesh, to Tarkovsky's latest films.

Imagination is inclined to find symbols in everything, and to transform everything into a symbol. From time immemorial, the most important parts of our body have been considered, and more than often worshipped, as symbols of the cosmic cycles: the genital organs, first, as they are connected with giving birth, then the heart, the lungs and the breathing apparatus, the sense organs, the limbs (and even the liver, as we have seen). Furthermore, somebody somewhere in the world has considered every single element or phenomenon of the natural world, from the tiny ant to the imposing mountain, from the regularity of the tides to the unpredictability of the storms, as a symbol of human experience. Poets have always been symbol-makers; from Romanticism on they have been doing it programmatically.

Gaston Bachelard (1884-1962) spent the first part of his life analysing the mechanism of rationality, starting with mathematics, and the rest of his life claiming for the imagination the status of a means for knowledge, just as important as reason. He did this by comparing myths, dreams, philosophy, and poetry under the light of a notion of imagination strictly tied to the four elements: water, fire, earth, and air. "The inner imagination of the vegetative and material forces" (1942: 12) involves us and is mirrored in our individual imagination, which recedes into itself to rework what it perceived, returning it back to the world in the form of a poetic act. We are called to an encounter by virtue of our human imagination, and the encounter occurs through the creation of symbols, which endorses the bonds between our psychic configurations and the dynamics of the elemental powers. In the realm of air, for example, we have the flying creatures, bird, angels, and various winged spirits, escorting the human psyche in dreams of flying and falling, and the poetics of the wind, the starry sky, and the clouds.

Therefore, Shelley discovered in the western wind the expression of the dynamic strength of the universe, creator and destructor, an alter ego to invoke to generate the song:

"Make me thy lyre, even as the forest is:
What if my leaves are falling like its own!
The tumult of thy mighty harmonies
Will take from both a deep, autumnal tone,
Sweet though in sadness. Be thou, Spirit fierce,
My spirit! Be thou me, impetuous one!"

(*Ode to the West Wind*, 1819)

His contemporary Karoline von Günderrode (1780-1806) saw herself in a "fragrant cloud", floating happily between the earthly world and the heavens, until, at last, beaten by a tormenting nostalgia, she melts into rain, giving herself to the realm of birth and death:

"So I cried,
I dissolved in tears,
I fell down
In mother's bosom.
Multicoloured flower-cups
Gathered all the tears
And I pierced
All the flower-cups,
I trickled down through the flowers,
Down and down
Into the womb
Of the veiled
Fountain of life"

(*Eistens lebt ich süßes Leben*, about 1805)

Sometimes, especially in the XX Century, poetic imagination has not been limited to picking an image from the external world (provided by the *fantasy*) and giving it a symbolic life, as in the examples above, but it composed complex and multilayered symbols, at times discordant, whose echo is vast and manifold, and hard to grasp. When Eliot writes "Garlic and sapphires in the mud / Clot the bedded axle-tree" (*Four Quartets*), he is aware of giving the reader an imaginative shock, and he will hasten to soothe it giving to the poem a conversational cadence, transforming the mudded axle into the centre of the cosmic wheel. And Paul Celan evokes the "breath crystal", the enchantment of the suspension of too much pain for death into a perfect shape, wonderful and far-off, being at the same time the purest quintessence of too much pain for life (*Atemkristall*, 1963).

However, the symbolic attitude is a double-edged weapon. On the one hand, it is the essence of poetic art; on the other hand, it can border on delirium. Sometimes we see all around us a web of symbols pursuing us (and a red traffic light can become a foreshadow of our existential catastrophe); sometimes we create symbols so twisted, introverted and tangled that they escape even ourselves, as well as others, eventually becoming dark and upsetting omens, confusing rather than clarifying. This happens when imagination is not acknowledged as it is, and it uses us, instead of being used by us.

For example, in its late development, the fantastic literature of Romanticism came to the verge of dream and nightmare, the farthest border of imagination. Many artists, especially in the final period, relied upon opium and alcohol as a way to trigger their imaginative resources, in an attempt to release them entirely from consciousness' control. Imagination becomes gloomy and morbid, and works are pervaded by a subtle uneasiness, which sometimes rears up in fits of anguish.

The exasperation of imagination ends in cancelling its mediation function (in more concrete terms: its dialogue with a shared reality), risking to become a deceitful comfort for life's pains, or a door for destructive powers to break in.

Once more, we have a precious suggestion in Blake: in his myth, imagination (embodied by Los) is able to accomplish its mission of rebuilding the fallen world, and reunite accordingly the vital principles of the human soul (the reintegration of the four Zoas), only if it is rejoined with its practical part (the Spectre) and with its feeling part (Enitharmon, Los' female counterpart).

Possible worlds

Let us say adieu for a while to our friends the magicians and the poets, and to "the land of infinity", and come back to earth, to look at the work of imagination in our everyday life.

Connecting past with future is necessary to find our way in the world. Such a bond is construed through simple associations of cause/effect (necessity), or through a more complex mental operation, in the scheme of if/then (possibility). Seemingly, both of these ways of anticipating events need no images. The former moves along a circuit which is not necessarily aware, and could be explained with some elementary mechanism of learning we share with our relatives the animals; the latter relies on a scheme of thought that can be expressed in logic and formalized with figures. Actually, imagination is the common ground of both: the child who learns that a punishment or a reward will follow a certain behaviour, construes a mental image of what will happen (a hug or a scolding), and will act according to such an image. She will also learn to arrange it: if a prank is too exciting, the image of the impending punishment will blur or soften up. The chess-player considering as many possible configurations as he can, caused by any single move, does not limit himself to construe schemes and algorithms, but he watches them develop in the chessboard of his mind.

The imaginative construction of the upcoming events tends to become, in a critical or emotional situation, a dramatic representation in all respects, either if we bustle about to foresee the attack strategy of the fanged tiger (or of the rival tribe), or if we prepare for a job interview. Also when the time of an amorous rendezvous gets near, in the thick of the jungle or at the pub near home. The fact that things may go in a different way from what we imagined (that reality projects a different movie indeed), is the complex and basically unpredictable essence of life (and, after all, what makes it liveable).

According to the French philosopher Paul Ricoeur, imagination is the matrix of action, "from the viewpoint of projects, from that of motivation, and from that of the very capacity to act". As regards the project, imagination is the place where we can virtually experiment with different possibilities of action, and anticipate any eventual progress of the situation. As regards motivation, imagination "provides the milieu, the luminous clearing in which we can compare and contrast motives as different as desire and ethical demands". As regards acting in itself, "it is in the realm of imaginary that I try out my capacity to do something, that I take the measures of 'I can'." (Ricoeur, 1976: 126). In imagination, I rework the images of the memory (the past), establishing action's potentiality (the future). It happens because imagination is an autonomous feature: it *is not* action, but "a free play of possibilities in a state of uninvolvement, where we try out new ideas, and new ways of being in the world" (ibid: 123).

Imagination is the ability to make up possible worlds.

At its lowest grade, it is what allows us to preview and to project the future, showing it in images. The more our imagination is mature, the more are the chances to find new and original ways to be in the world.

At its highest grade, imagination aggregates a universe of symbolic experience, which can manifest itself in the works of art.

But its key feature is always giving birth to a special level of reality, being on the one hand autonomous and separate from everyday reality; on the other hand, strictly bonded with it, retelling, reworking and transforming it.

In children's experience, the capacity to build worlds manifests itself with luxuriant grace in the dramatic play. There we can see how imagination not only provides the contents of the play microcosm (characters, scenarios, implicit or explicit rules), but it has also a pivotal role in the gesture that establish such a separate world and authorizes it to be alive.

As a legacy from the time I was into theatre for children, I still cultivate the pleasure, now and then, of telling stories. As a storyteller, I am of the dialogic kind: I encourage children to come into the story by putting questions, asking for sounds effects, even calling some of them to play a role. Therefore, I have a close relationship with the young listeners, and I had the chance to reflect upon some aspects of their way of being an audience. First, they are well aware of the necessary engagement: nothing less that the "intentional suspension of disbelief", which Coleridge posited as the necessary condition for meeting poetry (required also by the theatre spectator). It means entering a fictional world as if it was real, although provisionally. They know that they might meet something emotionally involving, and they prepare themselves to live it: the youngest ones look around to see a reassuring presence, to which they may quickly come back for comfort, in case of too intense emotions. Secondly, they know how to measure out the emotional involvement. When in the narration there are relaxed moments, sometimes with funny interludes, they are able to intervene with humour, also using the contrast of frames: "eh, he knew he was in a story!" But in the moments of climax, activating primary emotions (like fear) they want to stay with the story to the end. Of course, the youngest run to hug their mummy or daddy's legs, but usually they come back, after getting a supply of safety. This has always been the profoundest meaning of fairy tales: a safe place where children can store their negative emotions, but also go beyond them, embracing a message of hope.

We find this characteristic also in dramatic play. The act of make-believe implies the acceptation of an imaginative frame, endowed with coherence, autonomy, and flexibility, a "tiny little world" with its rules and its logic, even if these, unlike the real world, are liable to be changed by an act of will. Entering into this world means contributing to keep it alive, investing in it emotions and feelings. Emotions expressed in pretence play are real emotions. This happens because fantasy and reality do not entirely merge. It is demonstrated that two-year old children are able to communicate the difference between the two frames, and five-year old children can explain with many details how the two worlds work: they have a clear idea that magic works in Harry Potter's world and not at home.

However, the most interesting matter, shown by the thorough experimental studies of Professor Paul L. Harris, is the fact that the awareness of the frame and the emotional investment are not mutually exclusive: "preschool children can distinguish between reality and make-believe. They realize that an object that they can see is real and is open to inspection by others, whereas an imaginary creature is not, even if it arouses feelings of fear and attachment, and even if it has been part of their imaginative life for weeks or months" (Harris, 2000: 65).

When my daughter was five, she told me that under her bed the "devils of the dark" dwelled. They are not properly real, she said, but they are frightful all the same. (When, later, I asked her how it was going with her guests, she said they had left forever, maybe to relocate under a younger girl's bed). Children (and adults alike), Harris maintains, "despite a firm grasp of the distinction between imaginary and real situations, can be swayed in their emotional state by the contemplation of an imagined situation".

And he continues: "far from being a peculiarity of childhood, children's susceptibility to emotional engagement in imagined material is a characteristic of the human species throughout the life cycle, rather than a short-lived phenomenon of the early years" (ibid: 80). In Dramatherapy terms, this is defined as the attitude to *as if*, joining a cognitive aspect (frame discrimination) with an emotional one (the activation of real emotions in make-believe situations). It is the attitude presiding at children's play, and, in adult life, at the countless manifestations of the dramatic principle: rituals, festivals, and theatre. In the dramatic work, the strict connection of these two aspects permits the possibility to control emotional flow through the modulation of frames, introducing, for example, elements of "dramatic distance", or making interventions on the content, on the style or on the structure of action, which may lessen the emotional charge (or emphasize it, if necessary).

Imagination and relationship

We have seen that imagination is double-faced: on one side it is a temporary withdrawal into themselves, in the state of "uninvolvement" mentioned by Ricoeur; on the other side, it has a strong bond with the action, therefore an outward tendency; in any case, an emotional motion always accompanies it.

This quality of crossing the threshold between internal and external worlds ascribes to it a basic function in the process of relationship building. How does the idea of the other take shape within us, if not through an imaginative act?

The English psychoanalyst Donald W. Winnicott, in his attempts to explain the children's psychic world, bequeathed to us an appealing model, at the same time poetic and rich in heuristic resources. After weaning, children pass through a critical phase, with the difficult developmental task of establishing a distinction between themselves and their mothers, after a period of fusion begun in intrauterine life and continued in the lactation time. They therefore create a middle space, through a "transitional object", which can be filled with affects and emotions, standing for the mother although still being an actual object, yet endowed with a life of its own.

Like Gombrich's broomstick, I choose the teddy bear not because it resembles mummy, but because it can reproduce some of her features, like softness. Sometimes, it can take her place, and, for instance, reassure me in times of restlessness, but it can be also provisionally forgotten, neglected, and even punished. The transitional object and the transitional phenomena (similar but more primitive behaviours, like sucking one's thumb), are the first imaginative nucleus upon which play will rise up. But they are also the foundational act of the middle space between people, which Roger Grainger calls *betweenness*, at the same time uniting and dividing, the place that makes possible the I-Thou relationship, founding the sphere of interhuman. Only through this middle space, I can begin to conceive the relationship between me and my mother as a subject-subject relationship. According to Winnicott, however, the transitional object is not just a device to help us to cross a delicate developmental passage: it is at the very root of artistic creativity and spiritual sensitivity (Winnicott, 1971: 30).

Here we are back to Blake (and to Giordano Bruno before him): imagination is relationship.

In short: the process of individuation, which is the construction of our identity as a separated subject, begins in early childhood as an act of rupture of the primary fusion with the mother. It needs, to be bearable, a space of separation that is not a distressing void, but a place alive and throbbing, a middle space that sunders and connects. Imagination establishes such a "transitional space", enabling us to go beyond the primal split and to start looking at the other as a subject. Legitimating the others as separate subjects, creates a distance through which we can mirror ourselves in them, recognising what make us alike, and what makes us different. I construe myself mimetically upon the others, and turn back to articulate my mimetic fusions: this is a life-long process. Let us think of all the meaningful people we have met in our life, not only parents and closest relatives, but also of those we met later, in adolescence and after, and try to see how many traits of our person, either good or bad, have been retrieved from them, through a process of mimetic identification. And we are probably on the list of many of these people, some of whom are not perhaps on this earth anymore (and imagination keeps alive within us those who have left). The very act of acknowledging how the others' mimetic influences combine within us – and it is always a creative combination – allows us to understand ourselves as the ground on which a unique and unrepeatable synthesis is made. Such a synthesis is made possible by the middle space between me and the other, dividing and uniting, helping me to welcome the other with no fear of losing myself.

The others exist only if I can imagine them.

In the group artistic processes, like those activated by the Arts Therapies, the relational dimension of imagination is emphasized. The sharing of imagination, stepping together into the symbolic universe that rises when I open my imagination rooms to others' witnessing, or when I participate in a group creation where different imaginations meet, designs significant connections among people. Shared imagination manifests itself in dramatic, visual, musical, or bodily images. It is a vehicle to meet the others' world and to invite the others in our world, fostering our capacity to give and take. In Arts Therapies, this process is used to help subjects to recover their relationship abilities, which might be lost or damaged. These restored abilities will be spent outside the boundaries of the group, in the 'real world'. However, this does not mean that the group is a sort of gym, where you can train on a machine: on the contrary, the sharing of imagination with our travelling companions is a true and deep experience, nurturing and supporting us, and flourishing in the continuous making of our person.

13. Inner listening

Inner listening is the other pole of the *Inspiration* axis. It is something different from introspection, which searches for causes, connections, reasons; it is more similar to the attitude of a person beholding the sea: she is not interested in understanding how waves, winds, and streams work. At least, not for the moment. She lets instead the incessant movement of colours, sounds, smells and skin sensations fill her with their whole sensible universe, and go through her. When we turn toward ourselves with such an attitude, we must do it with devotion and serenity, silently and waiting.

Luvah

In Blake's myth, Luvah embodies the emotional side of human nature, in a range that goes from sexual love to affective bonds, going further to the emotion accompanying the spiritual communion. For Blake did not envisage any contrast between sexual and spiritual love. Living in a time when the appearance of decency inspired by an iron sex-phobia had to be maintained at all costs (even if under the counter the exploitation of prostitution, with the resulting business, was largely tolerated), Blake advocated the restoration of a lost Eden-like sexuality, and loathed sexual repression. "He who desires but acts not, breeds pestilence" *(Proverbs of Hell)*. Sexual repression is another of the "mind-forged manacles" that are imposed upon us, and we must get rid of them to expand our life. As S. Foster Damon has written, "Blake anticipated Freud by declaring that the greatest of social evils, war, is a product of the same repression" (1988: 368).

His Emanation is Vala, the natural beauty, contrasting and completing the quality of spiritual beauty embodied by Enitharmon (Emanation of Los-Urthona). In the fallen world, this contrast, distorted by a condemnation of females as tempters and seducers in a world ruled by a patriarchal despotism, makes her an outcast, accused of being the origin of all evils, while Luvah changes his passions to anger.

Luvah has a threefold manifestation: in eternity, he is the Prince of Love; in time, he takes two different shapes, seemingly contrasting. One is the fiery Orc, the revolutionary energy that transforms the world by destroying and regenerating it (like the Indian god Shiva). Blake had glimpsed such energy in the French Revolution, which had been betrayed by Napoleon's tyranny. The second form of Luvah in time shares the nature of Jesus, although in a different way from what we have seen about Imagination: there, it was the brotherhood among humans roused by the forgiveness of sin; here, Christ dressed with "Luvah's bloody robe" is the sorrowful Christ, expressing the common suffering of an oppressed humankind.

Orc is also the son of Los and Enitharmon, and this marks a deep connection with Los-Urthona (the connection between imagination and emotion). There are other elements suggesting this relation. Luvah is a weaver, and his labour mirrors Enitharmon weaving the vegetating world. His art is music, which is able to convey pure emotions, while the body part corresponding to Urthona is the ear.

From the point of view of the creative process, this connection suggests to us two arguments to reflect upon.

First, the creative act is always within an emotional circuit: in it are present the anxiety of waiting and the joy of the flow, the torment of doubt and the awe for the epiphany of something new. This emotional tone is present in the process as a whole, but it has a particular function in the inspiration axis, because (this is the second argument) the very stuff reworked and transformed by the imagination is emotionally loaded.

The creative process facilitates the encounter with our emotions, the emotion of now, and the emotions our story is made of. This encounter is a fundamental aspect of the *inner listening*, the complementary element to imagination, completing, in our model, the axis of inspiration. The creative process puts us in contact with our emotional world, but, at the same time, it works as a regulating principle: we are not overwhelmed by our emotions, but we enter into a dialogue with them.

Images and consciousness

The lengthy exploration of imagination in the last chapter has allowed us to sense its primary role in the creative process. Although in this part of the book we are dealing primarily with the artistic process, we must acknowledge that this occurs not only in arts, but also in every creative presence in the world, including science. Countless are the cases of scientific discoveries triggered by images: from the ouroboros, (the serpent eating its own tail) that appeared in a dream to the chemist F.A. Kekulé to suggest to him the structure of the "benzene ring", to the Shiva dance performed by a company of elementary particles for the physician Fritjof Capra, who derived from this experience the intuition that the most recent discoveries of microphysics can be fruitfully read in terms of oriental mystic doctrines. In the arts, its being a messenger between the worlds, upholder of the tongue of symbols, allows the imagination to move between the heart of the artistic process and it sources.

Which sources are we talking of? Where are the images that our *fantasy* fetches to deliver them to the work of imagination, which reworks, recombines, and reshapes them?

First, images are in things. They are in the objects of the surrounding world, perceived through the senses. Each percept becomes a mind configuration, which, according to the neurologist A. Damasio, has in the brain a precise match (the activation of specific areas of the brain cortex). "With the term image, I mean a mind configuration with a structure composed by elements of each sensorial mode: visual, auditory, olfactory, gustatory, and somatic-sensory. The somatic-sensory mode includes various forms of sense: tactile, muscular, of temperature, of pain, visceral and vestibular" (Damasio, 1999: 382). It is likely that our repertory of images (or at least the auditory and somatic-sensitive ones) begins to form even before the birth.

These images are stored in our memory, always ushered by an affective connotation, positive or negative (we tend to ignore the neutral ones). Not all the memory is aware: we have inexhaustible mines of unexplored images within us, seemingly forgotten or hidden, sometimes hazy and incomplete, sometimes astonishingly clear. They appear sometimes in dreams, odd association chains, and daydreams. This is the root of psychoanalytic psychotherapies and their techniques: dream analysis, free associations, and active imagination. They require from the patient the equivalent of what for the therapist is the "fluctuant attention" (see chap. 7), and they are used to help unconscious material to be analysed emerge. However, we are also talking about the modulations of our conscious control upon imaginative matter that each of us experiments with in everyday life. We can learn to use them to explore intentionally our secret storehouse of images.

This capacity of the consciousness to lessen its vigilance over the inner images, letting them surface and present themselves as emerging meanings, is an important feature of inner listening. Because images speak insofar as consciousness moves, and modulates itself to receive them: if it claims to be the master, they hide; if it withdraws, as in sleep, in hypnotic states and in trance, they become elusive and unfathomable.

Memory is not made only of images: it contains words, schemes, patterns, reasoning; much has been purposely stored (by heart), and it is easily retrievable with a voluntary effort; much has turned itself into automatisms, ways of being and of acting of which we are not usually aware, although they are liable to be inquired about. However, the deepest region of our inner landscape is largely made of images, painted with various emotional shades, which are reworked, reorganized, and re-signified by the part of our imagination lying beyond consciousness' threshold.

This "underground work" of imagination can have either a developmental or an involutional direction.

The latter occurs when imagination dissimulates, hides, or disguises the groupings of images that are connected with unpleasant states. Images remain unknown, but we perceive their influence as moods, vague yet intense sensations, and mysterious disturbances. Sometimes, for example when we remember -or we think we remember- dreams or fragments of them, imagination guides them across consciousness' threshold, in the form of symbols, which may appear ambiguous, upsetting and incomprehensible; nonetheless, at that very moment they become expressible. Expressing them through the languages of the arts, we can stand up to their power upon us, and this puts us in a safer position to begin knowing them if necessary.

The developmental direction is seen when imagination creates new configurations, manifesting themselves with the qualities of originality and surprise that are peculiar to creativity, altering our consciousness when they come into contact with it. Active (conscious) imagination continues the reworking process, bringing forth new images and new meanings, which are the very substance the creative process is made of.

However, images cannot come to light without a consciousness that modulates itself to meet them and authorizes them as possibilities of knowing: a forgotten dream is a lost dream.

To better define what we intend as consciousness, we turn again to neurology. Damasio identifies two kinds of consciousness, which he calls *nuclear* and *extended consciousness*.

They are founded, at brain level, upon the proto-self, "an interconnected and temporarily coherent collection of neural configurations representing the state of the organism, moment by moment, at different levels of the brain" (ibid: 212). Usually, we are not aware of the proto-self.

When this state is modified by the encounter with an object (being either an external object, including people, met through sense operations, or an internal object, brought by memory or imagination), then "the representation devices of the brain generate a nonverbal description, made of images, of the way the organism is modified by the elaboration of an object made by the organism itself and (...) this process intensifies the image of the causative object, putting it in a salient position in a spatial-temporal context" (ibid: 206). From the relation between object and organism, a level leap is produced: at the very moment when the presence of an object sets in motion fluctuations in my state configuration, I become aware of such a configuration. I become aware both of the object and of myself aware of the object. This primary form of consciousness, called "nuclear" by Damasio, rooted in the here and now of the moment, roughly matches with the rudimentary form of identity, which the cognitive psychologist Ulrich Neisser calls "the ecological self"[46]. It is already present in an embryonic form at birth, being the first distinction that children make between themselves and the world: the first sense of being an "I" in a specific place.

Focusing on our nuclear consciousness, feeling ourselves in the here and now, is an important starting point for the creative process. In terms of drama training, such a work is called "grounding": approaching our self-awareness through the awareness of our bodies, with their tensions and their energies, of the emotions going through us at this moment and of the environment. This helps to develop the basic attitude to creativity we have called *presence*.

Nuclear consciousness is connected with the fleeting moment, transitory and mutable like the water of the river, into which you cannot dip your hand twice. The extended consciousness is the river itself. It is the awareness that there is something before and after the present moment, that we have a past behind us, and (possibly) a future in front of us. This self-awareness, which Damasio calls "autobiographic self", keeps developing through the whole lifetime, starting from the third year, and it is the first nucleus of the representations of our identity we continuously build.

Stories

The latter form of consciousness is a rich and fertile land for the creative process, and it is another key object of the *inner listening*. Bachelard sees the very roots of poetry in childhood *rêveries*. *Rêverie* is a middle state between sleep and wake, allowing the free flow of images. And the images of childhood pervade the whole person of the *rêveur*. We are not talking about memory, which is "a field of psychological ruins, a junk-dealer of memories. All our childhood has to be re-imagined". *Childhood reveries* call upon the "persistence, in the human soul, of a childlike nucleus, an immobile infancy, yet always alive, out of history, hidden from the others, disguised as story when it is told, but being wholly alive in the instants of illumination – which means in the instants of its poetic existence" (Bachelard, 1960: 110).

And Rilke was writing the following words to the young officer who was feeling his poetic inspiration fading away amidst the insensibility of the military circles: "if between you and people there is no communion, try to be near things, and they will not abandon you; there still exist, not far, nights and winds, crossing trees and many lands; among things and animals everything is yet full of event, to which you are permitted to take part; and there still are the children as you have been as a child, so sad and so happy – and when you think of your childhood you live again among them, among the lonesome children" (Rilke, 1903: 43-4).

---

46   See Neisser, 1999.

This capacity to evoke, which is not only remembering, but rather getting close to the deepest imaginative nucleus of childhood, is an experience we all have had, kindled perhaps by the sudden recognition of a sense perception. The smell of an attic or of firewood, the taste of a biscuit (maybe dipped in a lime-blossom tea), a human voice, or a bird song, the soft sensation of cloth: all this may have granted us the shiver of an epiphany.

Listening to our extended self includes this kind of experience of reliving moments of our life, retrieving them emotionally and reworking them imaginatively. But we must turn also to the way our past has been re-imagined by ourselves, and is still re-imagined all life long: "disguised as stories".

Some years ago, a novel by the Brazilian writer Paulo Coelho had a good worldwide success. Its title is *The Alchemist*, and it is a story about a journey that is an initiation to life, searching for a mentor and then leaving him, coming to discover that what is to be followed is our "personal legend". Although many critics have blamed it for being too *New-Ageish*, lots of people like the book. Perhaps, they see in it the confirmation of an intuition they always had, never being aware of having it: that the life of each of us is a story worthy to be told, firstly to ourselves.

Because, all in all, we tell it anytime and anyway: the narrative dimension is what connects and gives sense to what otherwise would be a heap of sequences of events with no meaning. At the very moment I tell my story to myself, the biographic material takes the shape that I, as a narrator, confer to it; it colours it with the hues of my imagination, it takes new emotional shades. Incidents that in the past caused us to suffer, to the distant gaze they may appear as necessary passages for the story to go on. The same episodes, however, can be read as well as signs of a curse weighing on our story, felt sometimes as coming from a time prior to ours, and transmitted from one generation to another, like Cain's mark.

However, the remarkable point is that the overall narrative lying beneath our life is not written once and for all, and the moral at the end of the story is not a definitive one. Every narrative act opens the possibility of a change: if not of the actual facts, at least of the value we ascribe to them. Therefore, we can choose the right narrative style, the one that belongs to us in depth, and confers worth and dignity to our story. The choice of the style, which can be different in the various stages of our life, and the constant construction and assessment of our identity grow together: "narrative is not merely an appropriate form of the expression of identity: it is an identity content" (Eakin, 1999: 100).

Telling our stories, or listening to them told by other people, often provokes sudden insights on unknown, or not explored enough, aspects of ourselves. Similarly, imagining the other's point of view upon the story we tell is not only a narrative device, but also an inner experience generating an enrichment of meanings.

Archetypes

Finally, it happens that many of the images hidden in secret shrines, which are buried in the abysses of our memory, are special images, not coming from things, but from a memory which is vaster, deeper and older then our own They are images endowed with an intrinsic power, having a profound influence upon us; images that echo from age to age, and have manifested themselves in human creations for millennia. And they are witnessed in a myriad of symbols recurring in the spiritual imagination of peoples so far away from each other in time and space.

Jung has described some of these "primordial images", deriving his knowledge not only from his studies in myths and religions, but also primarily from having observed how they spontaneously surface into the consciousness at some special moments: those very moments marking transitions, inner transformations, and changes. In dreams and reveries of his patients, but especially in his own ones, which he describes with visionary power in *Memories, dreams and reflections,* written when he was very old (or at least old enough to feel untouched by the problem to give a veneer of scientific acceptability to his thoughts), Jung identifies the presence of some characters having the same qualities and function of those recounted in numberless stories, legends and myths. These figures are symbols of what Jung calls the *Selbst,* the deepest part of our souls, connected with the soul of the universe (the collective or transpersonal unconscious). The *Senex,* the elder wise man; the *Puer Aeternus,* the divine child; the Goddess Mother in her manifold forms: all these are figures of this kind.

In addition, the *hero,* the *helper* and the *antagonists,* actors of what Joseph Campbell, the greatest scholar in comparative mythology, called "the monomyth", the primordial mythical narrative unit, from which all the others are derived. And even the places being the stages of the journey to which the hero is called: the home, first, site of the hearth and safe point of departure, then the road and its many bifurcations, the mountain, the cave, the labyrinth, the far-off castle, the cosmic tree and all sorts of living beings, from dragons to centaurs, to talking animals. And even the funny donkey in *Shrek,* when it appears in our dreams, has got something to tell us, which is more profound than the amusing story we saw at the cinema.

The language we use to communicate with the archetypes is the language of imagination, and for them the same precautions we have considered while talking of symbols are to be taken. We must be careful not to take them in a superstitious way, as signs of a destiny, against which we can do nothing (as if we were characters in a story already written), but with the awareness that we are the players of this play. Only this awareness can allow us to recognise in them the voice of a profound inner wisdom, guiding us through the uncertainty of the passages.

We will not go further in the discussion about archetypes, and will not try to state whether they are psychic configurations connected with our genetic inheritance, or if they are transmitted by culture, or if they are not even to be considered as phenomena, but only as mere heuristic hypotheses, or if just thinking of them should be deemed a sign of insanity. Such a discussion has been developed by Campbell in his seminal essay on myth, *The Masks of God.* Nor will we try to find an order for these images, as attempted by the anthropologist Gilbert Durand (Bachelard's follower), who created a massive taxonomy of archetypal images in his book *The Anthropological Structures of Imaginary.* To go into these themes thoroughly, I recommend the above-mentioned texts.

As for the creative process, it is enough to mention how regularly such structures of imaginary have appeared in artistic products over the centuries, as well as in ateliers, workshops, and studios where the Arts Therapies are practiced.

These brief reflections on *inner listening* complete the axis of *Inspiration,* expressing the aspect of the creative process that develops entirely within us, although it draws out its materials from the external world.

We have seen how the key dynamic of the inspiration axis is the flowing of images. On one side, the harvest of our inner landscape, on the other side the function of imagination that manipulates and recombines internal materials with external perceptions, making up new configurations, which can be acknowledged and thought about.

The *Elaboration* axis, which we will explore in the next two chapters, concerns instead the shift through which these configurations, passing from potential to act, manifest themselves outside of the person, with others and for others.

14. Spontaneity

Tharmas

To begin our inquiry into spontaneity, the first element of the *Elaboration* axis, let us meet the character of Blake's myth we have elected as its patron.

Tharmas is the last of the four Zoas appearing in Blake's poetic pantheon, probably generated by the need to complete the quaternary of the principles ruling the human soul. He appears neither in the so-called *Minor Prophecies*, where Los-Urthona and Urizen are protagonists, nor in the former works (like *The Book of Thel*, where we meet for the fist time Luvah, as the Prince of Love). Being, so to speak, the youngest one, he is also somehow the most mysterious figure of the four. Nonetheless, his role in the mythic universe described in the three great "epics" of Blake's maturity (*Milton, Jerusalem*, and *The Four Zoas*) is noteworthy. If Los is "the fourth starry immortal", Tharmas is the first: "Begin with Tharmas Parent power. Darkning in the West". With this verse, in the First Night of the poem, Blake introduces us to the heart of the conflict. The Parent Power, shared by Tharmas with Enion, his emanation, embodying the generation instinct and Mother Earth, is the power that makes the couple the most ancient ancestors of humankind. It darkens because of the separation of the male and female principles (West is Tharmas' kingdom). The effect of this division is frightful: Tharmas, who in eternity is the exulting joy of the body and the senses open toward infinity, dissolves into the ocean, coming from time to time to the surface as stammering and confused instinctual impulses. Seeing such ruin, Enion can only intone songs describing the deadly aspect of generation, before vanishing herself in the Non-entity.

In his wholeness, Tharmas is the energy setting the world in motion, expressed at a human level in the glorious form of our body and in its moving. In the fallen world, this energy is debased in lower instinctual forms, like the survival instinct, which in human beings is the biological base of *Selfhood*, considered by Blake as the worst error, averting us from the awareness of our infiniteness.

Tharmas' job is sheep farming; his art is painting. These aspects are also worthy of mention.

The shepherd is a character present in Blake's world since *The Songs of Innocence* (1789). The shepherd becoming a piper and then a poet to write "a song of the Lamb" is the symbolic expression of a plain and unblemished life, concealing the figure of Christ "shepherd of souls", but he is also, as a part of the natural world, a serene witness of the universal cycle of life and death.

Painting, which is the art practiced by Blake in accordance with the Renaissance masters, in a fierce polemics against the meticulous likeness of the painters of his age, who "mock Inspiration and Vision", is, together with poetry and music, one of the "three Powers in Man of conversing with Paradise, which Flood did not sweep away".[47] For Blake, painting is Vision: art portrays in "minute particulars" what we see "not with the eyes, but through the eyes", because "If the doors of perception were cleansed, everything would appear to man as it truly is, infinite".[48]

Thus, Tharmas embodies a primordial psychophysical energy, joyful and exuberant: "Energy is eternal delight". The same idea that, two centuries later, the Welsh poet Dylan Thomas will envisage in "the force that in the green fuse drives the flower", and the philosopher Henry Bergson will acknowledge as the *élan vital*, guiding the evolution of living beings. It manifests itself in the generative and regenerative power of the *natura naturans*, in which our bodies and our senses partake.

Energy

Every process needs some energy to sustain it: *Spontaneity* is the energy of the creative process. Without its contribution, on the one hand, it would remain abstract and bloodless; on the other hand, it would be confined inside our mental boundaries. But it is also the element adorning and ennobling the creative process with its most astounding virtue, which is a freshness and a vitality that make it an experience of renewal and growth, even when the urge compelling it comes from pain. And, even though the process itself may go through gloomy moments, moods of anguish and uncertainty, or may meet failures and dead ends, spontaneity helps us to endure and face the difficulties, in the light of its intrinsic dynamism.

Of course, speaking of energy, nowadays, may sound a bit awkward (like the term "instinct" discussed in the introduction). The fact is that, for more than two centuries, the word energy has been the object of a drastic re-evaluation. The energy concept as stated by the physics (the attitude of a body or of a system of bodies to perform work, which can be measured and expressed in numbers), has become dominant, while we have been learning to exploit systematically the energy sources buried in our Earth, making ourselves more and more addicted to them.

Such a concept of energy, with the deriving corollaries (nothing can be created and nothing can be destroyed, but a part of the energy employed degrades to a lower form, more disordered and less exploitable), starts shaking when from the world of inanimate matter we turn towards life. That is to say, to those complex energy exchanges between an organism and its environment, including the transformation of such energy into the growth of individual beings. Life, it is told, is the only natural phenomenon contrasting the law of entropy (the principle of energy degradation).

When we move to the plan of our subjective perception of ourselves and others, when the energy we talk about is not physical or biological but mental, criteria become much more ambiguous and blurred. The fact is that we cannot but acknowledge in our energy state at certain times a substantial difference from the mere physical condition. The energy level we feel obviously has its roots in the "wellness" of the body, but it cannot be reduced to it, otherwise a healthy diet would be enough to overcome depression, and it would be hard to explain those people who show a great energy despite diseases or disabilities. The energy I own is the energy I feel. This kind of energy looks rather reluctant to be placed into customary

---

47 *Visions of the Last Judgement*, 1810.
48 *Proverbs of Hell.*

scientific categories: it is unspecific, non-measurable, often fluctuating; it looks as being able to regenerate itself, and its way to transform itself, to change direction or to dissipate is quite unpredictable.

All the models of the mind formulated in last Century had faced the need to assume some form of energy at the root of the psychic functioning. Whether this energy is the *libido* (sexual) of Freud or the *libido* (instinctual) of Jung, whether it is the "self-realization principle" of the humanistic psychologists, or even the "astral body" of the theosophists, I am not able to tell, and perhaps it is not so crucial for our inquiry. Therefore, we will not investigate further the ultimate nature of psychic energy, but we will try to see how it is released in the creative process, in the form of *spontaneity*.

Theatres of spontaneity

In the twenties of the last century, a young physician of Romanian origin, Jacob Levi Moreno, founded in Vienna a company of improvised theatre, beginning the journey that was to take him to invent psychodrama, the first psychotherapeutic technique using dramatic tools.[49] The company was called *Das Stegreiftheater* (the theatre of spontaneity); in its extemporaneous performances, Moreno identified the embodiment of the *S Factor* (the spontaneity principle, strictly connected with creativity). What moves the actors when they improvise is a sort of instinctual energy, described pragmatically by Moreno as "the force pushing the individual to search for an adequate answer to a new situation, or a new answer to an old situation" (Moreno, 1923: 6). In his enthusiasm, he came to the conclusion that liberating the spontaneity, through improvised drama, is the first step to becoming the creators of ourselves, which is the ultimate purpose of human life. According to Moreno, the *S Factor* is inscribed in human subjectivity: it is present since early childhood, and it does not depend on learning. Education, in fact, tends to hinder spontaneity, replacing it with "cultural preserves".

"The state of spontaneity", he wrote in those years, "is not permanent, fixed or rigid like written words or melodies, but is fluent, of a rhythmic fluency, rising and falling, ascending and vanishing as the acts of life, yet it is different from life. It is the productive state, the essential principle of any creative experience" (Moreno, 1923: 134).

When, many years later, Moreno tried to fix a permanent theory of spontaneity, he stepped into the inescapable problem of the need to resort to concepts like instinct or psychic energy to define its nature, and he ended up making the idea quite blurred and elusive. Nor were his attempts to make up tools to assess and measure the spontaneity (according to the prevailing fashion of psychological tests in the USA, where he took refuge to escape Nazism) more successful: his *Spontaneity test* has almost fallen into disuse. However, Moreno's happy intuition that spontaneity is a key psychic feature, potentially belonging to each individual, remains as an important trail marker. With, as a result, the idea that it can be reawakened, even if it has been stifled by a coercive education or destroyed by pain, through specific training.

---

49   And probably the first group psychotherapy.

Improvising

The first attested use of the term *spontaneo* (spontaneous) in Italian language dates back to the Middle Age. It means, "what one does by his own impulse, with no constraint or request from others"[50], which is the same meaning of its root, the Latin adverb *sponte*. If spontaneity refers to the production of an action in absence of external stimulations, then the actual spontaneous acts, entirely driven by an internal urge, are quite infrequent.

Perhaps, they do not exist at all, as since our birth, and even before it, we are immersed in a world made of connections and mutual influences between us and our environment (including people), of which we are not always entirely aware, a web of interactions within which our actions are constantly set. The infant cry is the spontaneous expression of discomfort; such discomfort, however, can be related to nourishment, so once more with a world of relationships.

Our actions are placed into this flow of relationship. In this sense, Moreno's definition of spontaneity as an answering capacity may appear a truism. However, spontaneity manifests itself not only in the action of answering to an environmental stimulus: a spontaneous action presents a particular quality.

The most evident aspects of such a quality are immediacy, appropriateness, and naturalness.

When children's play is at its best, in its "state of grace", these aspects of spontaneity are clearly visible. I recall some long play sessions with animal puppets, between my daughter Viola and a friend of hers, when she was five-years old. Every gesture, every move of the game was in the right place, where it had to be, with no hesitations or regrets, as if the two children were following a detailed script, including adventures, relationships and feelings played by the puppets. Nor did they take time to prepare it: a simple agreement between two characters ("I am the rabbit and I call on you…") was enough, and the rest flowed without any effort, leaving the daddy-observer with a sensation of freshness and vigour. The explanation my daughter gave of the inexhaustibility of that play was that "animals are alive".

These aspects of spontaneity are evident in all the developmental phases of the children's dramatic play between the second and the seventh year. According to the well-known EPR paradigm (enunciated by the dramatherapy pioneer Sue Jennings), the children's dramatic play passes through three phases, called *Embodiment*, where play expresses itself primarily through the body; *Projection*, where children use toys, puppets and other objects; and *Role*, where they act as characters (make-believe play). The creative attitude, which has grown since the first day of life, with the continuous effort to discover the world experimenting with it, manifests itself brilliantly in the spontaneity of dramatic play. It begins with the first "running play" described by Peter Slade, the joyous run celebrating the achievement of the upright position, to the free dances, the made up songs, the action of giving voice to a puppet or a title to a scribble, and the pretence of being a dog or a pirate.

Slade maintains that *Child drama* is a form of art, and as a form of art it should be studied. If we take into consideration again the structure of the artistic process we identified in the Introduction (training, improvisation and composition), we will see that, in dramatic play, improvisation and composition coincide. Children create in the moment they act.

---

50   Cortellazzo – Zolli, *Dizionario etimologico della lingua italiana*, Zanichelli, 2000.

In what we usually call Art (with a capital A), these three structures have been considered for a long time as rigidly separate: the artist learns the language, experiments with it, then uses it to realize a project. Improvisation in most of the cases is just in the service of training: a case in point is the method of Kostantin Stanislavskij, the Russian director who has been considered the founder of modern theatre. Revolutionizing a conception of the actor as a repository of a prearranged repertoire of roles, Stanislavskij proposed a strategy of progressive approaches to the character, introducing improvisational structures (like the "as ifs" and the "given circumstances") in setting up the performance. However, here improvisation is still serving composition.

To find, at least in the Western world, some forms of art in which the two structures overlap (like in children's play), we must turn to the second half of the century, after two wars and a deep cultural sea-change. From the Fifties onwards, especially in America, countless artists had ascribed to improvisation the nature of creation tout court: from Jackson Pollock's *action painting* to the dancing improvisation of Anna Halprin and her *Dancer's workshop*; from the theatre improvisation of Keith Johnstone and Viola Spolin, to the extraordinary flourishing of jazz improvisation, which, through various stages (called from time to time *be-bop, cool, new thing* or *free jazz*), endorses the phenomenon of a work of art which is created by the moment.

All these art forms share some conditions, stated by the philosopher Davide Sparti in his essay on jazz, which may also be extended to any form of improvised art. "1. Inseparability. The act of composition and the act of performance are inseparable. (…) In improvising, the creative process and its results occur at the same time. 2. Originality. Any improvisation – namely every act of composition/performance – is (more or less) different from the previous acts of composition/performance. 3. Extemporaneousness. Improvisation is an extemporaneous activity (…), living in the here and now, without the benefit of written music as a guide in the arrangement of notes (the past does not control the present and the future). 4. Irreversibility. The composers can cancel a wrong passage. The improvisers cannot; neither can they, the day after, play again – but better – the same piece, nor correct themselves. 5. Responsivity. Improvising implies not intention, but rather attention, the ability to react to the changes introduced in the course of music, which pairs the ability to take decisions influencing the direction of the music itself" (Sparti, 2005: 118-9).

In all these art forms, training is crucial. In jazz, for example, improvisation is possible only on the basis of a perfect knowledge and mastery of the instrument. However, jazz training is not a formal teaching as in academies: we only have to think of the countless jazz masters who were autodidacts. Likewise, the training of theatrical improvisation is basically interactive: it is practically a series of improvised dramatic games set in an order of increasing difficulty. This makes us reflect on the fact that creativity training is a creative process itself (we will come back to the argument later, in chapter 17). In any case, in improvised art, it is necessary to have a very specific skill of the medium that is used. Based on this skill, spontaneity manifests itself in its wholeness in the improvised artistic gesture, revealing the same aspects we have recognised in children's dramatic play: immediacy, appropriateness, and naturalness.

I will attempt a brief exploration of each of these aspects; referring to the arts I know best: theatre and music.

Immediacy. The spontaneous action appears as a motion from inside to outside which is not planned, denoting an ability to act without a predefined project, and even without the mediation of thought. This seems to contradict what we have said before about the relationship between imagination and action. If every action is imagined in advance, how can such immediacy exist? However, the time of consciousness does not necessarily correspond to the time of imagination.

We can find a possible explanation of this process in an interesting trend of research of neurosciences. The brain wave called LRP (Lateral Potential Readiness), appearing in the brain cortex when a person projects a motion, is present 500 thousandth of a second before the action, while the awareness of the decision (TCA: Time of Conscious Awareness) is formed 200 thousandth of a second before the action itself.[51] Our brain and our central nervous system are able to set up a scheme of action in a split second, even before our *nuclear self* can record it. The intervention of the consciousness may stop the action or modify it, but the image of the action precedes the actual decision to act.

The actors or the musicians improvising have no time to consider consciously all the possibilities: they act relying upon the impulse of the moment, letting the imaginative schemes, born under the threshold of consciousness, guide the action. They must learn to trust them, and to take the risk.

Appropriateness. The levels of expressive freedom allowed in improvisation are related to the structure of the improvised work. In theatre, three levels are usually identified. The first (structured improvisation), provides a roughly predetermined sequence, within which actors have room for variations, embellishments and deepening (acted for example through monologues), but they remain anyway within a fixed plot. The second level (semi-structured improvisation) is built around general directions (for example a theme, a setting or some fixed roles), but the development of the plot and the relationships among characters are made up during the improvisation. The third level (free improvisation or impromptu) is indeed entirely extemporaneous: actors come onto the stage with no idea of what they will do, and they let the performance grow from the interactions on stage. In jazz we have a similar pattern: jazz improvisation ranges from written pieces leaving enough space for improvised solos, to the use of standards (themes usually very well known, used as guides), to the total improvisation of free jazz.[52]

Yet even when freedom is at its height, the result is not a formless hotchpotch, a juxtaposition of loose sounds or gestures; it appears instead as an organized chaos, a meaningful event. This is because in improvisation – in any kind of improvisation – every expressive micro-event (gesture, word, action, or sound) is always connected with the others. Such connection may manifest itself with different nuances, according to the internal rules of the groups of improvisers: they may be either equal or governed by a leader; they may stress either on challenge or on support; in any case, they move along a dialogical principle, rooted in a continuous sharing. Give and take: accept the other's proposals and offer yours.

In group improvisation, such connection implies a particular sensitivity to grasp even the smallest hints from the others, including involuntary body signs, which are shown in posture,

---

51   Libet et al., 1983.
52   It is worthy of note that many jazz giants had made a journey that led them to cross the three levels in different stages of their artistic life, like John Coltrane, Miles Davis and Ornette Coleman.

muscle tension, and facial expressions. It also implies the ability to rework them at once to calibrate our action. We find again the dynamics of attention we have analysed in chapter 7: the improvisers must be focused on themselves and on their own action, but at the same time, they must be aware of anything happening around them.

From the subject's point of view, "appropriateness is the feeling that our own actions and reactions are not false notes, but they belong to a harmony of the relationship; they are fitting to the context and, meanwhile, they contribute to its construction and definition" (Pitruzzella, 2004: 95). Jonathan Fox (Moreno's follower, inventor of the *Playback Theatre,* a form of psychosocial drama based on improvisation), suggests that the idea of appropriateness may "include a difficult-to-attain notion of 'right action', not unlike the Zen master's injunction to 'eat while eating, sleep while sleeping" (Fox, 1986: 80).

Naturalness. What is the meaning of the last phrase? At first sight, it just looks like an invitation to follow our natural body needs: eat when you are hungry, sleep when you are sleepy. Indeed, this invitation goes much further, asking us to live our actions, even the most trivial, with the awareness of the present moment. The musician Keith Jarrett, author of many performances of total improvisation, some of which are to be considered absolute masterpieces, maintains that "creativity is the awareness of the potential of the moment" (Toms, 1997: 91)

In his well-known report of a western thinker's encounter with the world of Zen Buddhism, Eugen Herrigel has outlined the fascinating paradox lying underneath the practice of archery (*Kyudo*). On the one hand, the aspiring archers submit to an intense and laborious training; on the other hand, they can succeed in hitting the target only when all this is forgotten, and the archers become one thing with their bows, their arrows, and their targets. Then the archer's task is just to let the arrow go, and it will get the target by itself (is perhaps the arrow also alive, like Viola's puppets?).

Although the expressive act of the improviser is the fruit of a long process of learning, at the very moments it comes to life it seems to flow without effort, tending to essentiality. We can see nothing in it that is either factitious or superfluous, the same sensation as watching the elegance of a cat when it moves.

We can conclude this chapter affirming that spontaneity has a double role in the creative process: it is the energy sustaining the process, which expresses itself in searching and experimenting with continuously new forms; but at the same time, it is the energy pushing the process towards its accomplishment. We will see in the next chapter how this push meets with the last function of our fourfold model, so completing the elaboration axis.

15. Productiveness

Scores

Examining spontaneity, we have considered how the creative process stretches out to reach the world. In improvisation as an art form, which has served us to identify its distinguishing traits, we have seen that the creative act manifests itself through perceptible forms. They are perceptible not only by the authors/performers of the improvisation itself, but also by an external observer. The fact that these forms are ephemeral, not retainable except through reproductions (like the recordings of the jazz jam sessions), does not exclude their being complete forms. In their way, they are definitive forms.

The American poet Gregory Corso has written precious verses for the musician who perhaps has been the greatest jazzman of all time, Miles Davis:

> "Your sound is faultless
> pure and round
> holy
> almost profound
>
> Your sound is your sound
> true & from within
> a confession
> soulful & lovely
>
> Poet whose sound is played
> lost or recorded
> but heard
> can you recall that 54 night at the Open Door
> when you & Bird
> wailed five in the morning some wondrous
> yet unimaginable score?"
>
> (*For Miles*)

Corso grasps the quality of wholeness and authenticity of the art of Davis (who at that time was beginning an extraordinary life long process of creative experimentation); conversely, he testimonies the uniqueness and the impermanence of the moment. There are no known recordings of that session at the *Open Door,* nor could we travel back in time to relive it. Yet we know that a creative event came to life on that night, generated by the musical imagination of the artist (*Your sound is your sound*), which met with his inner listening (*a confession soulful*

& lovely). This meeting took shape under the impulse of spontaneity: what Miles and Bird (Charlie Parker) have done is not *playing*, but *wailing*, which is the term used by the Afro-Americans to speak about their music, made of *mood* and *jam* (improvising). However, the poet adds an intriguing particular: that the result of this *wailing* is a *score:* an *unimaginable* one, and certainly not repeatable, but with no doubt a score, a complete work, at last until we can tell this story.

The tension towards the actualization of forms, toward a result of the creative process embodied in an object/event, which marks the closure of a creative cycle (but also the possible beginning of another one), is the major characteristic of *Productiveness*. Examining this tension, we will face a crucial issue of the creative process: the relationship between expression and communication. We will try to explore this issue as carefully as we can; but first, let me introduce the *Zoa* patronizing productiveness.

Urizen

The figure of Urizen is one of the most relevant and powerfully described in Blake's pantheon. In the *Minor Prophecies,* he contrasts Los, embodying the aridity of the abstract reasoning when it is severed from imagination. It mirrors the diffidence shown by the young Blake for the incoming industrialization, which induced him to a bias against science as a whole (in a time when science was taking its first steps to self-electing as the only way to know the world).

Eventually Blake showed his appreciation of the possibilities of reason dialoguing with the Poetic Genius: Urizen manifests itself as a demiurge able to make up worlds of admirable proportions, the architect who built the pyramids and the gothic spires. In the *Four Zoas*, Urizen accomplishes his cycle from fall to rebirth passing through various stages. The philosopher Sergio Givone has written: "Urizen, prince of light, falls into the abyss; he parts from Ahania, who is the telluric and female principle. While in their union Urizen and Ahania represent knowledge in the form of truth (that is the immediate communion of finite and infinite, and of reflection and action), when they are separated, Urizen becomes empty philosophy and Ahania remains unsatisfied desire" (Givone, 1978: 107). The fallen form of Urizen is Satan, the demon presiding over the cycles of civilizations: their rising, flourishing and self-destroying. Invoked by the dying Albion as a remedy for his internal chaos, Urizen proclaims himself as the only God "from eternity to eternity", and begins his creation, in which we see the evolution of productive thinking from the geometric harmony of classic architecture to the frightful death machines of the war industry. Urizen's project to raise himself as God, mastering the other Zoas and repudiating Ahania (who, as female principle might allow the humanization of science) leads him to destroy the universe he himself had created (the *Mundane Shell*). The Prince of Light turns into the Dragon of War.

Urizen's rebirth, in the final Night of the poem, begins when Albion calls him for the second time: "Come forth from slumbers of thy cold abstraction come forth / Arise to Eternal births!" However, this time man is prepared to receive the gift of reason: Los, with the help of Tharmas, has built Golgonooza, the city of art (imagination reconciled with the body), and Luvah has manifested himself in the form of Christ (passion turned into compassion). The regenerated Urizen resumes his role of cosmic farmer: he ploughs the universe, spreads the human seed, gathers the crops, and threshes them, pulling apart peoples and nations. Doing so, he inaugurates a new era of humankind that has learned not to impose itself on nature's cycles, and is able to ally itself with them, respecting their sacredness. His final rejoining with Ahania represents the recovered union of science and wisdom, and the overcoming of the conflict between rationality and creativity.

In the development of Blake's thought, Urizen ceases to be the sheer rationality to which his name is tied (it derives probably from "your reason", where "your" refers both to the reader and the poet himself, and also to the ruling rationalism of the Age of Enlightenment), becoming a more comprehensive principle of realization. The poetess Kathleen Raine, who was a sharp exegete of Blake's art, maintains that the name of Urizen may have its origin in the Greek term *oùrizein,* meaning "to limit" (from which the word "horizon" derives). The etymology is controversial (it is not certain that Blake knew the ancient Greek language as early as 1793, when he first mentioned Urizen); nonetheless it is quite fascinating. In this sense, he represents the indispensable limit of the creative process: its necessity to be fulfilled within the boundaries of the interhuman.

Realization

In the novel *The Night of Saint John,* Mircea Eliade tells the story of a painter who has only one canvas, upon which he paints a subject over another, overlying many strata of paint. Yet none of these works has ever been seen by other eyes than his. One day, the painter decides that the time has come to show the picture to someone worthy, and invites the woman he loves in his secret space. He makes her sit down, and he removes the cloth covering the easel. The woman's reaction is of disappointment: "It is all black!" As we may imagine, the love story is not going to have a successful conclusion: what we glimpse in the character's behaviour, the expectation that his lover would be able to sense his hidden depths, challenging her to prove her love in this way, shows clearly the immaturity of his feeling, his incapacity to love.

From the point of view of art, however, the story suggests to us a further consideration. The painter has lived the creative process in all its elements (imagination, spontaneity, inner listening, and productiveness) in each picture he painted, exactly like Miles in that night at the *Open Door.* Moreover, he has been, at every moment of the process, the only witness of an ephemeral work, which will soon be covered by another, renewing a continuous creative process. At a personal level, the author is satisfied with his work. The problems come when he feels the need to share his world, which he has tried to put upon that canvas, with another person, who has not been involved in the process. The encounter is impossible, because the product is formless and bears no traces of the process, even if we look for them with a rational gaze rather than with an emotional one. The secret remains a secret. The attitude of the woman (the audience) cannot but be one of detachment.

The arts work when they allow others to relive the process with the author, or at least they do not hinder them. This happens when the author keeps the other inside herself. It does not means that artists, while creating, must foresee the eventual response of the audience, nor even that they necessarily must have an audience at all, but it outlines the fact that there is no art but within a relationship. Which is, after all, primarily a relationship with oneself: the first painting by a child (a slap of pap over the tablecloth or something similar) is art in this sense. The form engendered by the creative gesture lives at the very moment we make it and we perceive it. Growing within the sphere of interhuman, a possibility opens that our creative gesture is dedicated to the other. Calling their parents as witnesses of a drawing or a dance, children renovate the covenant of giving and taking by the artists and their public.

The production of forms in the creative process obeys thus two different needs, one towards ourselves, and the other towards ourselves and others (and towards ourselves *as* the others, in a world of vital sharing). In the development of children's creative function, it moves from the first to the second, from a personal to an interpersonal level, which can become, in some cases, a social level. Perhaps, the difference between what we call art and children's play is all here: in play, the first level is in charge, the level of the spontaneous joy of the creative process. It develops integrating the second level, as children make their way in a world of relationships. In art, the different levels, personal and interpersonal (social), are usually coexistent.

In Arts Therapies, the process is usually nearer to play. The product of the expressive work is addressed on the one hand to the author herself, who can assume the double role of performer and witness, putting herself at one step from her own work; on the other hand, to the group sharing the process (including the therapist), which mirrors in it, reflecting it back to the author. From this sharing, in some cases, a need can emerge in people to propose the outcome of the process to an audience beyond their playmates (through an exhibition or a public performance, for example), the need to turn towards the *general other*, besides the *significant other* (to use the expressions of the psychologist G.H. Mead). In the best cases, this need is accompanied by the awareness of a transformation that has occurred through the creative power of art, and by the decision to bear witness of it to themselves and to others.

The personal level concerns expression; the interpersonal level concerns communication.

Expression and communication

Expression, as the etymology itself suggests (*ex-premere*, pushing out), refers to the external manifestation of an internal moving. When what is inside comes outside, it completes and defines itself.

A classic example is the expression of emotions. An emotion is always accompanied by involuntary somatic events, involving our neuro-vegetative system. This somatic activation has the tendency to manifest itself in physical forms (body and face attitudes) and immediate actions (like laughing or crying). These expressions are also involuntary, but, unlike those bursting out of the autonomous nervous system, they can be kept under control. If I meet a lion in the forest, the adrenaline that is secreted by my suprarenal glands is out of my command, as well as the cold sweating and the increasing of the heart pulse, and even the rising of my body hairs. I cannot control all these occurrences enough (so the lion will perceive my fear anyway), but I can avoid shouting and running, which may have a catastrophic outcome. However, generally the suppression of the emotional manifestations is connected with cultural constraints or personal difficulties, and is not so handy for survival: indeed, it often makes life more complicated. When I express an emotion, the effects of this expression on my self-perception make a difference, a cognitive shift that preludes the possibility of an aware elaboration; conversely, the unexpressed emotion cannot be fully known.

The more the internal motion is primitive, the more immediate will be its expression. The primary emotions have codified cultural forms of expression. However, expressing more complex emotions, which include contradictory aspects, needs an imaginative passage: *Odi et amo* (loving and hating) can only be expresses in poetry.

Whichever the internal motion may be, its expression facilitates its integration into the person's balance. But the person does not exist in a void: she encounters others and continuously confronts herself with them. In a world of relationships, the nature of expression is to tend towards the other, to address itself: in other words, to become communication. And communication demands a code. There is no universal code: they are always cultural conventions, which can even be shared by small groups (which may later be adopted by larger ones, and eventually by the society as a whole, as often happens with artistic avant-gardes). I am able to evaluate a product if I understand the code, but the code is not made only of organized signs; it rather includes a series of aspects concerning the context, within which the communication occurs, like the relationship between the maker and the receiver of the act of communication itself. When my three-year old son showed me a drawing made of overlapping spirals of all colours, saying that it was "the belly of the whale" (from *Pinocchio*), in my judgement the appreciation of the intensity and originality of the work and the delight of seeing the rising of the creative passion in a person I loved, were at the same rate. In the groupwork in Arts Therapies, the code is built up together, and, on the basis of this sharing, everybody is given permission to acknowledge the process within the product and appreciate it, seeing the person behind the creative effort, and being mirrored in her.

Communication is usually defined as a transmission of information from a source to a receiver through a medium. Within this impeccable general definition, we must take into account the complexity of the information concept. The verb "to inform" has the same root of "form". Information always transforms the subject who receives it, in ways that are different both in degree and in substance. In the sphere of the interhuman, engaging in a communication is an experience within which any exchanged information modifies the condition of both the subjects communicating.

The Italian educator Danilo Dolci emphasized the fact that communication has the same root as "communion"; to communicate is to share (in this sense, the mass media can inform, yet they can never communicate). The child doodling is satisfied of what she is doing; but when she takes her piece of paper and shows it to her mother, she is communicating not only the content (look what I have done), nor only her commitment (look what I can do), but she is asking no less than the permission to exist. "The permission to exist", wrote the psychologist Felice Perussia, "is the acceptance of spontaneity. It is the activation of the person in the sense of facilitating their natural disposition to be actor-author. It is developing, or rediscovering, the natural ability to accept or to refuse the proposals of the world" (Perussia, 2000: 275). The mother observing and letting herself be involved with that doodle is giving such permission, and, at the same time, she is giving herself the permission to exist as mother. Their exchange is an act of communion, confirming the primal condition of being together, but it attests, conversely, the possibility of being distinct individuals.

In the Arts Therapies, the activation of the creative process occurs within a relational frame. Most of its applications are done in a group; indeed, the group is an important resource for the process to be accomplished. However, even when therapy is individual, the aspect of communication is still important. The role of the therapists is also of participating witnesses of the subject's expression; according to the dramatherapist Robert Landy, they must "embody the creative principle and mirror it, to return it back on the client" (Jennings, 1992: 110).

While in many areas of our lives, expression and communication are separated, in the creative process they are joined in a single gesture, even when subject and object of communication is the same person. Although the creative act is made in solitude, and dedicated by the author to herself, in it the other is contained (another individual, a specific group or a homogeneous ensemble of people, or even the whole humankind).

This affirmation poses two questions worthy of note. They are engaging questions, touching on the old unresolved controversy on the ultimate nature of art, to which we will not attempt to find answers (perhaps because there are no definitive ones, and, if there were any, we would miss out the opportunity for many interesting conversations).

The first question is: is it possible to talk of creativity (or even of art *tout court*) when the process halts at the expression stage, never becoming communication?

The second is: if the process is instead living within a circuit of communication, how the responses of its communications influence the process itself and its possibilities of development?

All that we could say is that every creative process is set at a point of a continuum between the two manifestations of the *Productiveness* element; a point which can be different in every single act. Yet every point participates in both of the aspects: I can either express for myself and communicate to the world, or express to the world and communicate with myself. Expression and communication are like the Yin and Yang of the Chinese philosophy; in the middle of the Yang there is a small part of Yin and vice versa.

The creative process reaches its full scope when I can see in it the accomplishment of a project, being either aware from the beginning or revealing itself in its products, a project that might be pre-existing, or it might take shape in the course of the process. This occurs both when the creative product, as provisional as it might be, is the synthesis of what I needed to express, and when, in its incompleteness, it incites me to go further, when it poses questions rather than providing answers.

With this treatment of *Productiveness*, our examination of the four elements interacting in the dynamics of the creative process is concluded. We have noticed how these elements are autonomous, in the sense that any of them has its own characteristics and can be present even in absence of the others, but also that they are interconnected and interdependent in the process, although not necessarily ordered along a precise sequence.

In the next chapter, we will see these connections closely.

16. Into the game

It is time now to turn back to our scheme, and use it to put in order the mass of ideas and information of the previous chapters, which have provided us with a wide and varied enough picture, but with little cues on their relationships inside the process. I propose it again, for the reader's convenience.

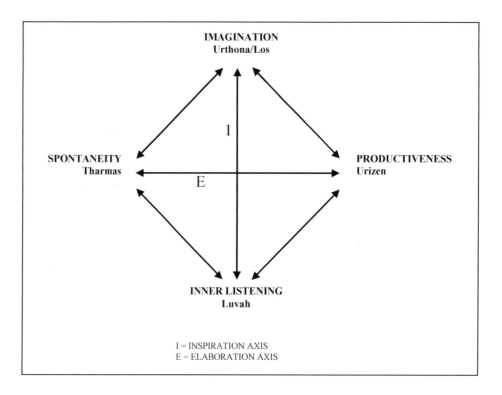

Figure 5: Elements of the creative process

The central circle represents the area of the creative process. The two crossed axes of *Inspiration* and *Elaboration* show the connections among the elements of each axis with the elements of the other. Connections engender other meaningful axes, describing polarities that, if they are in a dynamic balance, denote the vitality of the process. To analyze them, I borrowed models of logics and semeiotics (See Appendix 2).

Secondly, the diagram suggests the possibility that the dynamics of inspiration and elaboration can flow through different patterns, according to the sequence with which the elements are activated along the process.

Lastly, we will examine the risks that the creative process runs when one of the elements is absent or underdeveloped, or when an element overflows, dominating the whole process and reducing the space for the others.

Polarities

We can consider Imagination and Inner listening as complementary, as synergic factors of inspiration; similarly, the two elements of the elaboration axis (Spontaneity and Productiveness) are complementary too.

Imagination needs the material provided by the inner listening; it needs to be in contact with the riches of our world of emotions, feelings and stories, to remain not mere *fantasy* (in Coleridge's sense), which goes in the direction of denying the world, rather than being a tool to meet it. Inner listening needs imagination in order that its contents can be seen and acknowledged. In the continuous conversing of the inspiration elements, the seed of the productive necessity is contained.

Spontaneity needs productiveness to preserve its energy from being dissipated in a confused entropic stammering, yet indeed, it can be made concrete through the making of forms. Productiveness needs spontaneity to introduce a principle of free research and experimentation, which may keep it from becoming only the cold execution of a project.

The elements imagination and productiveness are contrary, in the sense that they cannot be simultaneously present: seemingly, if I am engrossed in imaginative thinking, I cannot produce at the same time. Similarly, inner listening and spontaneity are contrary: the former reminds us of stillness, of the rest that accompanies us into ourselves, the latter of the dynamism projecting us towards the world.

Spontaneity and imagination are contradictory, in the sense that one looks like excluding the other: if an action is spontaneous, obviously it cannot be imagined in advance. In the same way, inner listening and productiveness are contradictory: the former seems addressed to the interior of the person, the latter to the outside.

The creative process makes possible the harmony between opposite tensions. According to M. Csiszentmihalyi, "(creative people) contain contradictory extremes – instead of being an 'individual', each of them is a 'multitude'. Like the colour white that includes all the hues in the spectrum, they tend to bring together the entire range of human possibilities within themselves" (Csiszentmihalyi, 1996: 57). Moreover, we have seen how the tolerance of ambivalence has been commonly considered as one of the basic traits of the creative personality (see chapter 4). It derives, as our brief analysis of the contrapositions among the elements has shown, from the fact that at the core of the creative process there is a dialogue between our internal and external worlds, along which our experience unfolds.

In the rhythm of the process, such dialogue manifests itself as an alternation of stillness and motion. This polarity suggests to us that the creative process is not a continuous flow: at some moments it springs with ease, at others it slows down, or even stops. Sometimes it seems to feed on its own effort, and therefore long periods of fruitful activity are sustainable; at other times it is in a period of rest that new ideas come, which will push the process further. The image is of an artesian well: when it is full, we can get lots of water; then we have to wait for the waters from the depths to fill it again. The creative rest, as Wallas had already noticed, is a fundamental part of the process. "Rest before Labour", is the epigraph that Blake puts at the beginning of *The Four Zoas*.

But the dialogue inside/outside implies a more primary dimension of the creative process, legitimating it as a meeting space for the different modes of experience, which are at the root of our very identity. In the creative act, I create an in-between world, a special level of reality, where my inner world melts with the external one. In the universe of the creative act, they are not separated. Yet at the same time, the intentionality of the creative act itself establishes a clear boundary: though bearing signs of my inner world, the object/event of my creation is actually outside, and I can contemplate it at a distance.

Creative styles

The spark that kindles the creative process can be found in any of the elements: its position will determine the trend of the process. Different trends are related to different creative styles. The creative style is the way our creativity accords with our personal features, with our specific strategies for encountering the world.

The *locus nascendi* of the process may be an element of the inspiration axis: imagination and inner listening.

In the former case, the sense images (generally visual or auditory, but also somatic-sensory), which are formed within us, colour themselves with emotions; in the latter case, memories, emotions, feelings come to the consciousness' surface, and they ripen into images. Then, in both cases, images look for their way to manifest themselves in the outside world through the elaboration axis. We can call the first *imaginative style*, and the second *inner style*.

However, the creative process can be triggered also by the elements of the elaboration axis: spontaneity and productiveness.

In the former case, actions, motions, sounds, which are either perceived or produced by ourselves, even by chance, gain meaning as they turn into images having an emotional tone, and they strive to find forms to express themselves. This is the *spontaneous style*.

In the latter case, problems or projects appear in our minds, they develop with the contribution of the inspiration axis, and they are realized through progressive experimentations. We can call it the *productive style*.

We find all these possibilities in artists' legends. If I am Mozart, I can hear in my mind, while taking a walk, a whole symphony, and run back home to transcribe it. If I am Proust, I can evoke a childhood memory, and make an entire humanity spring from it. If I am Keith Jarrett, I can put my hands on the keyboard at random, and develop these sounds until they become the sublime *Köln Concert*. If I am Bach, I can plan to compose thirty variations upon a theme I had written as a keyboard exercise, and create the immense *Goldberg Variations*. If I am just myself, I can play with all the creative styles, and enjoy the various challenges and delights that they may offer.

Balance and imbalance

The dynamics of the creative process can be described as an alternation of balances and imbalances; each imbalance generates a new balance, which in turn unbalances, and so on. Even the final balance of the object/event closing a creative cycle can become the question from which a new cycle starts.

The emergence of a dominant element at a certain point of the process, creates an imbalance, which is counterbalanced by the contribution of the complementary element (as we have seen above), but above all by the contrary element.

Productiveness, the urge to reach an object/event provided with a form, can stem the overflowing of imagination. Similarly, the imagination contrasts a productiveness that is exclusively founded on rational thinking, preventing it from becoming "cold abstraction".

Inner listening, inviting us to retreat into ourselves, indulging in the contemplation of our inner landscapes (with the risk of getting deeply entangled), is counterbalanced by the spur of spontaneity towards action. Likewise, spontaneity is restrained from becoming purposeless excitement, and gains meaning if it can drink from our inner well.

When the imbalance in the creative process is caused by the momentary prevalence of one of the elements (at the beginning of the process or during its course), it produces motion pushing the process forward.

However, the imbalance can indeed be the consequence of the underdevelopment of one of the elements, or even of its absence. In this case, it tends to be fixed, blocking the dynamics of the process rather than fostering it and can jeopardize the whole process, as a counterbalance is missing. Thus, it can happen that the missing element is replaced by its contradictory one.

So when the productive drive is missing, it happens that the creative process, not able to find a way to the outside, curls up around itself, growing dim among the shadows of the internal world. When, conversely, the gates of the inner world are closed, productiveness asserts itself in arid and impersonal constructions.

When spontaneity, the day energy, is lacking, imagination may come to be believed to be self-sufficient, feeling no need anymore to face the world. But when imagination, the major mediator between the worlds, is limited or absent, action takes command; an action which does not acknowledges the boundaries between inside and outside, constantly upset by the soul's motions not coming to expression.

This last condition, the lack of imagination, is the most serious as regards the fulfilment of the process. Fortunately enough, it is also the easiest to recover and cultivate. However, even the other elements, when inadequate or absent, can be reactivated if the process is wisely led. Similarly, it is possible to intervene when the natural counterbalancing of the elements is blocked and one of them overflows, engulfing the whole process.

Here, we enter right into the contents of the next chapter, which will explore the effects of our model on the roles and functions of people called to lead creative processes (including their own).

17. Leading the creative process

Although in my life I led hundreds of creative groups, in different areas, I still get thrilled every time I start a new group. It is quite a strange emotion, combining aspects that are absolutely normal, like a slight self-consciousness at being centre stage, with a particular feeling, of excitement and risk at the same time: the awareness of being on the verge of a journey, but only knowing the point of departure. A process can be set in motion and governed, but its outcomes are always unpredictable: originality is a basic feature of creativity, and what is original questions our knowledge categories and our abilities to forecast.

Given this premises, in this chapter (which concludes the part of the book on the creative process), we are going to briefly explore some issues related to the role of the guide of creative experiences, either in therapy, or in education and professional training. Despite the differences, we can identify some common traits, and use the models we have discussed before to support the awareness of guiding such experiences toward their purpose, which is fostering creativity in individuals and in groups.

Contexts

However, though the purpose is the same, the functions we ascribe to the growth of creativity in the three areas above mentioned are very different. In therapy, creativity has a transformative function; in education, a developmental function; and in adult training an enhancing function.

Therapy. The therapeutic area is a vast and multifaceted area, concerning all those situations where suffering of any kind, either of the body or of the soul, turns into a call for help. In general, I feel quite comfortable in saying that a creative approach can be good almost everywhere. For example, it has been shown in recent years that the introduction of play in children's hospitals has improved their efficiency, even in a strict medical sense. Moreover, the use of Arts Therapies has successfully started to spread in unexpected fields, like the healing process of serious illnesses such as cancer or Alzheimer's disease. However, there are two main sectors where the creative approach seems to have a well-established tradition. The first is the psychiatric area, where the application (more or less judicious) of arts to healing has a long history, often underground and sometimes overtly dissenting with the ruling medical practice.

Many of those experiences of the arts as a factor of humanization of a system, which has been since its origins an instrument of exclusion, rather than of care, are considered to be the ancestors of the present-day Arts Therapies. The second, more recent, is the area of supporting people with learning or physical disabilities in their development and in their social integration.

116

Sometimes ago, telling of a Dramatherapy journey in a Therapeutic Community, I wrote: "I believe that inpatients largely share the awareness that they are in that place neither to be withdrawn from circulation and forgotten (as occurred in the old asylums), nor to be re-educated into a world that has been too hard for them to bear. They are there instead to be accompanied in rediscovering and enhancing their personal and social resources, which may help them to construe a meaningful experience in that world, even if it might be necessary to come to terms with their illness. Yet such project can only be founded upon an indispensable premise: that they take their responsibility to be active subjects of the healing process. And this is perhaps the most delicate and difficult point that the mental health professionals have to face day by day: rousing, in people who are withdrawn, focussed on their own discomfort and often frightened, a lively attitude of participation" (Pitruzzella, 2007:174). The unique contribution that a creativity-oriented work can give in this sense is to facilitate people's capacity to affirm their role as subjects, reappraising their own resources; subjects who are able to transform the world and themselves. Through the awakening of creativity, people open to change, and to the courage of being; working with others and sharing with them their own imagination, they break their shell and begin inventing new ways to be in the world.

Education. Differently, in the field of education, the importance of creativity has always been recognised from the prevailing pedagogic thought, at least since Pestalozzi (in the Age of Enlightenment). Until nowadays, many scholars have stressed the need for a creative education. Unfortunately, these ideas have been practiced only by virtue of willing individuals or groups rather than becoming a widespread culture. The very teaching of artistic languages in schools is quite often more technical than creative, encouraging reproduction rather than invention.

The list of advantages of a creative education, as regards the making of the children's personalities, their learning abilities, their socialization, and their psychophysical wellbeing is endless. We will not attempt to propose it here, also because it would imply repeating many of the things we have said in the second part of the book. We will only say that creativity is not just an added value in a normal working school, to preserve it from a boring routine and from a dangerous tendency to conformism. Conversely, it has revealed itself as a precious tool to support it in critical situations, for example, when integration issues are present, or when systems of negative relationships (of aggressiveness, exclusion, and bullying) in the classes jeopardize their functioning.

Training. A last area in which the creative approach has a story of its own, although brief, is adult training, especially in the professional field. In companies, the creative approach is aimed at innovation and problem-solving; it has been used lately also to improve interpersonal relationships and sustain the groupwork abilities, preventing mobbing situations. However, it is in the professions above mentioned that the awakening of personal creativity can have extraordinary effects on a professional plane. Not only because people can experiment with patterns that can be proposed to their groups of students or clients, but mostly because they learn to look at their own job as a creative art, living and throbbing, never boring because it is always new. They learn to trust their own intuition, and to find new answers to old questions.

Tasks

In my book *Introduction to Dramatherapy*, I compared the dramatherapist to a person looking after a fire. "He has to arrange paper and firewood of various sizes: the thin and dry twigs that easily catch fire and generate an intense but fleeting heat; the middle-sized branches, wrist-thick, which guarantee a strong and continuous flame; and finally the logs, that will be enduring nourishment for the fire. He has to make the first spark glow, and he must blow, softly or strongly, to sustain the newborn little flame. He has then to watch it and to keep it in balance: to add firewood or to move it to make it flush, or to remove the logs to slow it down. Finally, he has to gently let it extinguish, preserving the embers for the next day" (Pitruzzella, 2004: 124)

I think this image can refer indeed to all the Creative Arts Therapies practitioners, and, more generally, to all those guiding creative experiences. It emphasizes the tasks of this particular kind of role: setting up the conditions to activate the process, and, most of all, taking care of it.

To pursue such kinds of tasks, a clear awareness is needed of the context: of its constraints (space, time, and rules) and of its opportunities; of the subjects' difficulties and resources. On the basis of this awareness, it is necessary to formulate hypotheses and foresee eventual developments, build up tools to observe the process purposefully, and assess its outcomes.

Such scientific attitude, which is indispensable in addressing the creative process to its functions of transformation, development, and enhancement, requested by the contexts, is however not enough if we do not consider a crucial fact: guiding a creative experience is in itself a creative experience.

A person guiding creative experiences must possess the virtues of clarity and levity; she must know how to put herself at the right distance between being part of the process and understanding and directing it. Accordingly, we have to resort to our personal creativity: whatever being the context in which we operate, our duty is to cultivate and to refine it, trying our best to apply it in our individual life, both as an artistic practice and as an everyday approach. "The internal creative artist must be fed: it is a good habit for the dramatherapist to practise at least another artistic discipline besides the theatre (and not necessarily connected with it), as well as to enjoy all the arts. But also to gaze at the sea or at the clouds, the bugs or the rocks; to play with a cat or with a child; to grant himself moments of idleness and of what Gaston Bachelard called *poetic reverie*" (Pitruzzella, 2004: 132).

Our internal artist suggests to us both the attitudes to keep toward the processes we master, therefore toward the main actors of such processes, and the tools we may use to understand them, adjust any imbalance, and lead them to well-deserved happy endings.

Attitudes

Those we have identified in the first part as "the emblems of creative attitude" (*Curiosity, Versatility* and *Presence*), may help us to describe clearly enough the ways the leader must cope with the process, in terms of meeting the experience, coming into contact with it, and living it. The aspects through which the three emblems manifest themselves may provide us with some advice.

Curiosity. Openness is the attitude of turning towards others considering each of them as a unique and precious subject, as they are the holders, in their own special and unrepeatable ways, of the creative principle. The other person is not only someone to care for, to help or to educate, but an active and creative protagonist of her own process of growth and transformation. This does not lessen the significance of our role as therapists, educators or trainer, or even our responsibility, but it is rather an invitation to be receptive, ready to question our ideas about what is good "for them". Looking at the other person (my client, my student or my trainee) as a creative subject induces me to trust her potentialities and her resources; and it will be mirrored in the self-image of the subject, fostering self-esteem and motivation. Finally, all this has to be sustained by a sincere capacity for wonder, which means also being able to notice the minute particulars, hints of expression or tiny signs of something moving, and to welcome and appreciate them as events, even before ascribing to them any meaning or value.

Versatility. Such a suspension of judgement, invoked as a requirement for wonder, finds its most mature expression in what we have called "diversification of viewpoints". It implies our ability to identify ourselves with others, in order to grab their perspective, eventually coming back into ourselves to understand it. It is a confrontation with multiplicity, which cannot, and must not be avoided, although it might bewilder us. It is here that tolerance of ambiguity becomes important: a person leading creative processes must be able to cohabit with doubt, aware that it can be necessary, sometimes, to linger in the chaos, maybe just enough time to "generate a dancing star". And all this has to be done by keeping a sense of lightness and playfulness.

Presence. The quality we have called "intensity of experience" reminds us that guiding the creative process involves an undivided participation in the process itself, with our desires, our emotional states, and our feelings. At the same time, it is necessary to distance ourselves, to maintain a diffused attention, which permits us to perceive all that moves around us, both in the centre of the scene and on its margin. The attention dynamics described in chapter seven may help us to understand this singular paradox: a person leading a creative process must bear testimony personally on what it means living for the moment, but she must be able as well to make choices addressing the future. The last component of Presence, aesthetic sensitivity, is the background of the whole process: it is what allows us to penetrate and fully savour the ten thousand languages through which creativity expresses itself.

Tools

It must be stated beforehand that all the above listed qualities of the creative attitude (with the exception, perhaps, of wonder) have been theoretically inquired, and often experimented with, by many psychology scholars[53]. It would seem possible, consequently, to build scientific enough tools to assess and evaluate the level of this or that single component of creativity.

---

53   The monumental *Encyclopaedia of Creativity,* lists at least 80 different tests to assess creativity (Runco, Pritzker, 1999: 755-60).

Furthermore, in the context above mentioned, the improvement of creativity can be assessed through its fitness to the context's purposes, whether being of transformation, development, or enhancement.

Potentially, we have at our disposal an extraordinary range of instruments to evaluate the results of creative processes in terms of outcomes. Nothing is however available to help us to read the process in its making, nor even cues about what to do when we take the responsibility of leading it.

If "the emblems of creative attitude" had provided us with some direction about the general approach to the process, the elements we have identified in the third part may suggest us some tools to observe and manage the process itself.

First, we must be aware that our *creative style* will influence the process. If I am predominantly of the imaginative type (or interior, spontaneous or productive), I will tend to focus the process around the element that is most consonant with me, with the risk of minimizing the others and setting in motion an unbalanced process.

Being aware of our personal style, we should nurture the contrary element, to counterbalance the prevailing one, to ensure the solidity of the process. Yet we must not forget that it is our privileged tool for understanding.

The author of this book, for instance, having precociously discovered that his style is an imaginative one, inclined to dream and *reveries*, for a long time has forced himself to do handwork, designing and making wooden objects, until he introjected the sense of the work done, materially visible in the tree-house or in the cat's bed. This has maybe helped to prevent the risk of a certain vagueness, intrinsic to imagination, permeating through his whole work as leader of creative processes. Nonetheless, he knows for certain that at difficult moments, imagination will stretch out its hand and point to the answers (and it has done many times, while writing this book).

Now, let us look synthetically at the resources that each element, balanced by its contrary, may offer us in terms of comprehension and guide to the action. This time, we will begin in the opposite direction, compared to what we did earlier, starting with the elements of the Elaboration axis.

Productiveness. We have already stated that the product of a creative process is a new and suitable object/event, which is the fruit of the transformation and regeneration of pre-existing elements. The pathway of a large creative cycle, like those activated in the context we have examined, is pointed with such products, being either accomplished objects/events of artistic relevance, or simply new ideas, attitudes and viewpoints. Yet the product of the whole cycle (an overall increase in the creativity of individuals and groups), is at a qualitatively different level. In a sense, it is more elusive, as we cannot identify it with specific objects or ways of behaving. It may happen, conversely, that actions and objects made in the process are not very convincing, because we do not understand them, or because they do not fit our aesthetical criteria. Nonetheless they are, in a mysterious yet unquestionable way, steps on a journey leading to the growth of creativity.

In this, which can be called the *creative meta-process*, the general objective is attained through a series of single processes: it is the development, in the subjects, of a function that can implement more of those processes, triggering a virtuous circle, which eventually will establish itself as a permanent trait of the person.

However, if this meta-process, for the leader, is still a creative process, it is also evident that the relationship with the product is of a completely different kind. As we have said before, productiveness is the tendency to generate forms, which are put at some point of the axis "expression-communication". Observing them can be a source of either delight or torment, yet there are forms standing for their authors, of whom the author can say: it is mine. In the guide's thankless task, there is the paradox of putting aside our subjectivity to foster the other's, implying self-control, which, sometimes, may seem inconsistent with the creative flow, yet it is necessary to avoid the risk of overlapping our creative needs (as well as our aesthetic inclinations) with those of the subjects, influencing them too much: this is the fundamental ethical rule to remember.

However, even if, as guides, our self-expression is limited, the emotional impact with the product (the growth of creativity) is absolutely identical: we experience the same joy as the artist, when the product is well-made, and the same restlessness when it fails.

In our productiveness is inscribed an intelligence of doing, allowing us to foresee sequences apt to actively recombine the elements of the process, in an order that may foster a gradual development of the creative abilities of the subjects.

The creative opportunities proposed (in forms of training exercises, improvisation cues, and themes for compositions) can be ordered according to their level of complexity, or emotional intensity; they can be spread in a balanced way, considering which of the elements is more present; they can be organized to alternate moments looking towards inner life with others action-oriented.

Yet the most interesting aspect of the role of productiveness in the creative process is its enrichment when it contacts its opposite: imagination. This meeting brings forth a global image of the process, which appears as a harmonic whole, when the events follow each other describing a unique pattern.

Spontaneity. To keep this creative flow alive, it is necessary to know how to measure intervention and make choices. Sometimes, for example between a session and the following one, we have time to reflect upon the process, assess what has happened and address the following interventions on this basis. However, often we need to take a decision on our feet, in the course of the action itself, to overcome hindrances that may block the flowing of the process, and limit any excesses that may lead it to dead ends. Such choices are to be made straight away, although they are delicate ones, which might turn the whole process' direction, given the influence of our role as guides. Our only chance is in trusting our spontaneity.

Like jazz improvisation, as we have commented in chapter 14, spontaneity has to be construed in time, with enduring craft, by observing, examining, and experimenting with a large amount of creative processes. The more our spontaneity is ripening (that is, using Moreno's words, when our *S Factor* awakens), the more our intuition of the instant becomes effective. And each happy intuition reinvigorates in its turn our own spontaneity.

It can be useful to take note of our spontaneous choices, to try to penetrate their sense as much as we can, increasing our awareness of the deep reasons suggesting them. We will then discover how great is the role played by our own inner guide in such choices.

Inner Listening. In the whole field of the "helping relationships", the first thing to learn (even if nobody teaches it) is the way to understand and use our emotions. This idea is intentionally applied in the training of psychologists, psychotherapists, and educators. It is still overlooked, unfortunately, in other professions, which would receive a great benefit from it (like teachers, physicians, nurses, social workers, and so on). It is definitely emphasized in Arts Therapies, as they handle highly emotional stuff: the artistic expression.

Listening to our own emotions as signals to grasp the sense of the moment, or using them to enter into an empathic contact with others: these both are vital functions of inner listening for the person leading creative experiences. Similarly, it is indispensable to keep our emotions under control, to avoid them overflowing and influencing the process.

Yet there is another aspect of inner listening, subtler but nonetheless important in our job of guiding creative experiences: the fact that our innermost feelings act as catalysts of other people's creativity. This implies another paradox: that the more we dwell into ourselves, the more we are able to stay into the flow. When this happens, and the marriage of inner listening and spontaneity is done, then emotions, feelings, stories, and symbols populating our inner landscape enter into contact with those of the subjects, and form an alliance. From our inner horizon, elements are rising and becoming alive, accompanying the process through the mediation of imagination.

Imagination. The quality of imagination, which assists people leading creative processes, is the one we have defined "relational imagination", recalling the primary act of construing the other within us, as the fulcrum of the dialectics between mimetic fusion and individuation. This kind of imagination engenders the vision of change, helping us to hold the wheel in a journey, which is ever-changing and unpredictable.

I will try to expound such a complex concept with a simple example. A few years ago, the Israeli dramatherapist Mooli Lahad wrote a precious little book, in which he explains a series of imaginative techniques used to supervise various kinds of practitioners (especially arts-therapists, psychotherapists and social workers). One of the techniques is the following: try to think of one of your clients, who arouses your concern. Then close your eyes and imagine that, during the night, an angel comes down from heavens and kisses his forehead. The following morning, the problem has gone. What is the first sign, the first minute particular pointing to the transformation? Furthermore: can you remember a moment when you have actually seen such a tiny sign, or something similar? When did it happen? What caused it? Could it recur again? Here, Lahad suggests, "we are at the fist step of the transformation ladder" (Lahad, 2000: 61). The sequel will be a work of thought, which, starting from the remembered moment, tries to understand "the subsiding mechanisms of the wished behaviour".

At the core of this exercise an articulate imaginative play stands. It starts with a stage that, in Wallas' model, can be defined as "preparation", namely the focusing of a problem. The problem, however, concerns not an object or an abstract entity, but rather a real person, with whom we have a real relationship. This implies the evocation of an image, our image of the person in question, and the activation of an emotional flow (otherwise, we would not be "worried"). When we close our eyes, the components of imagination (images and related emotions) are already moving: the awakened imagination portrays a figure, which not only reproduces the traits of reality, but also reveals its potentialities. Then it brings us back to reality as the place where such evoked potentialities can come true, inviting us to devise strategies which are always new.

The tool of imagination may open unforeseen routes in understanding what we do when we propose creative processes to people. In our role as creative guides, it has to be connected with productivity, which allows us to turn it into a project.

These suggestions, taken from the creativity model expounded in this book, certainly do not cover all the issues of our role as guides in the above-defined context. They may however provide some space for reflection upon the ways of harnessing our own creativity to "care for the fire" of creative process.

The book, at this point, has no reason to go further. The following volume will try to provide the reader with practical cues, taken from the repertory of Arts Therapies professionals. Meanwhile, I hope that you, dear reader, who had the patience to get this far, may reason upon the proposed models, and find new connections in practicing your own creativity. And I hope also that you may use them to create new tools to meet and know your "mysterious guest" and its wisdom.

Epilogue: On being creative in times of destruction

An old legend tells of a man standing on the ocean's shore. He is not fishing, nor does he dive in search of pearls: all he does is telling stories to the ocean, which listens enthralled. Yet this man is held in great esteem by his people, because they know that if he stopped telling the stories, or if he was silenced, no one could tell what the ocean would do.

(adapted from Carrière, 1998)

Appendix 1

Blake's Four Zoas

Name in Eternity	LUVAH	URIZEN	THARMAS	URTHONA
Quality	Emotion	Reason	Instinctual Energy / Body	Imagination
Emanation	Vala (Natural Beauty / Nature)	Ahania (Intellectual pleasure)	Enion (Generative Instinct / Earth Mother)	Enitharmon (Spiritual Beauty / Inspiration)
Name in Time	Orc	Satan	Covering Cherub	Los
Zoa (Bible)	Bull	Lion	Eagle	Man
Sense Organ	Nose	Eye	Tongue	Ear
Body Part	Loins	Head	Heart	Legs
Metal	Silver	Gold	Bronze	Iron
Position	Centre	Zenith	Circumference	Nadir
Element	Fire	Air	Water	Earth
Cardinal Point	East	South	West	North
Occupation	Weaver	Ploughman	Shepherd	Blacksmith
Art	Music	Architecture	Painting	Poetry

(From: Pitruzzella, 2007)

Appendix 2

The logical squares

The creation of the so called "Square of oppositions" (see figure below), which outlines the mutual relations among the four categories Aristotle used to order any possible statement, is traditionally (although probably by mistake) ascribed to the Byzantine scholar Michael Psellos. A proposition can be universally affirmative (Every man is good), denoted with the letter A[54]; universally negative (No man is good), denoted with E; particular affirmative (Some men are good), denoted with I; particular negative (Some men are not good), denoted with O. Putting them in a square, the fundamental logic relations are highlighted. A and E are *contraries:* they can be both false, but they cannot be both true. A and O, as E and I are *contradictories:* if one is true the other must be necessarily false. I and O are *subcontraries:* they can be both true but not both false. A and I, as E and O are *subalterns:* A implies I, as E implies O (but not vice versa).

A thousand years later, the Lithuanian semiologist Algirdas J. Greimas used the square to investigate the microphysics of texts, not only the verbal ones, but any set of signs carrying a meaning. Starting from the structuralist reading of myth[55], which sees it as a narrative mediating opposite tensions, Greimas portrays, with an elegant variation of the "Psellos' square", the possible configurations generated by the development of a nucleus of contrasting fundamental values (see figure below). The oppositions can be quantitative (contrary axis): good/bad; privative (contradictory axis): good/not-good, bad/not-bad; participative (complementary axis): good/not-bad, bad/not good. Greimas denotes the elements of the square with the letter S, standing for *seme*, the minimum unit of meaning. For example, the opposition black/white engenders not-black which could be "light", and not-white (Not-S_1), which could be "dark".

But if we consider more complex oppositions, the possibilities of generating sense multiply. Let us take for instance the opposition being/appearing, which generates not-being and not-appearing. In this case, the relations among the elements of the square produce further sense configurations, structured in oppositions in their turn. Being and appearing produce the concept of truth; not-being and not-appearing the concept of falsehood; being and not-appearing the concept of secret; appearing and not-being the concept of deceit. It is different indeed if we oppose to being (instead of appearing), the term becoming: so, the couple being/becoming produce the notion of life; not-being/not becoming that of death; the axis being/not becoming confers a sense of immobility, while becoming/not being a sense of motion. In addition, if we observe the other two possible couplets (being/not-being; becoming/not-

---

54   The affirmative propositions are denoted with the two vowels of the Latin word *affirmo;* the negative ones with the two vowels of the word *nego.*

55   See Lévi-Strauss, 1958.

becoming) we will find some synthetic descriptions of two existential dilemmas, present in literature from Hamlet to Peter Pan. And so on. In this way, Greimas construes a structure that can be used to fathom out the sense of any story, and, as we are made of stories, can become an intriguing game to describe the functioning of the mind.

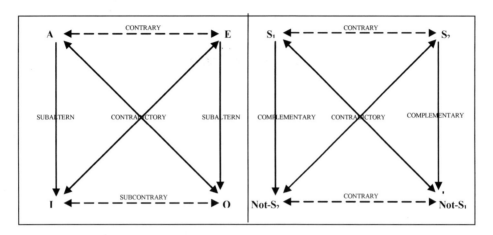

Psellos' and Greimas' squares

Bibliography

Abbagnano N. (1979) *Storia della filosofia*, 3 voll., UTET, Torino

Aczel A. (1996) *L'enigma di Fermat*, Il Saggiatore, Milano, 1998

Amabile T. (1983) *The Social Psychology of Creativity*, Springer-Verlag, New York

Amabile T. (1989) *Growing Up Creative*, C.E.F. Press, Buffalo (NY)

Amabile T. (1996) *Creativity in Context*, Westview Press, Boulder (CO)

Anderson H.H. (a cura di) (1959) *La creatività e le sue prospettive*, La Scuola, Brescia, 1972

Antonietti A., Cerana P., Angelini C. (1994) *Visualizzazione intuitiva. Risolvere i problemi con "L'occhio della mente"*, Franco Angeli, Milano

Arieti S. (a cura di) (1959-66) *Manuale di psichiatria*, 3 voll., Boringhieri, Torino, 1969-70

Arieti S. (1976) *Creatività. La sintesi magica*, Il Pensiero Scientifico Editore, Roma, 1979

Bachelard G. (1942) *Psicanalisi delle acque*, Red, Como, 1992

Bachelard G. (1943) "Immaginazione e mobilità", in: *Il mondo come capriccio e miniatura*, Gallone editore, Milano, 1997

Bachelard G. (1943) *Psicanalisi dell'aria*, Red edizioni, Como, 1988

Bachelard G. (1960) *La poetica della rêverie*, Dedalo, Bari, 1972

Bailey D. (1980) *Improvisation. Its Nature and Practice in Music*, Da Capo Press Inc., 1992

Baltrušaitis J. (1972) *Il Medioevo fantastico*, Adelphi, Milano, 1973

Baron-Cohen S., Harrison J. (1996) *Synestesia: Classic and Contemporary Readings*, Blackwell, Oxford

Baron-Cohen S., Harrison J., Glodstein L.H., Wyke M. (1993) "Coloured speech perception: is synaesthesia what happens when modularity breaks down?", *Perception*, vol.22, pp. 419-426

Barron F., Montuori A., Barron A. (eds) (1977) *Creators on Creating*, Tarcher/Putnam, New York

Bassi A., Santoni Rugiu A. (1969) Creatività e deprivazione artistica, La Nuova Italia, Firenze

Bateson G. (1979) *Mente e Natura.* Adelphi, Milano, 1984

Bateson G. (et.al.) (1952) *L'umorismo nella comunicazione umana.* Cortina, Milano, 2006

Bateson G. (et.al.) (1956) *"Questo è un gioco".* Cortina, Milano, 1996

Bateson G. (1972) *Verso un'ecologia della mente.* Adelphi, Milano, 1976

Bateson G., Bateson M.C. (1987) *Dove gli angeli esitano*, Adelphi, Milano, 1989

Becchi E. (1963) *Appunti per un'educazione alla creatività*, Industrie Grafiche A. Nicola e C., Milano-Varese

Bendin M. (1990) *Creatività. Come sbloccarla, stimolarla, svilupparla e viverla*, Mondadori, Milano

Bergson H. (1907) *L'evoluzione creatrice*, Laterza, Bari, 1957

Blatner A., Blatner A. (1988) *The Art of Play. Helping Adults Reclaim Imagination and Spontaneity*, Brunner/Mazel, New York, 1997

Bocchi G., Ceruti M. (a cura di) (1985) La sfida della complessità, Feltrinelli, Milano

Bocchi G., Ceruti M. (1981) *Disordine e costruzione. Un'interpretazione epistemologica dell'opera di Jean Piaget*, Feltrinelli, Milano

Bogen J., Bogen G. (1968) *Creativity and the Bisected Brain*, in: Rothenberg, A., Hausman C.R. (eds.), 1976

Bogen J., Bogen G. (1999) *Split Brains: Interhemispheric Exchange in Creativity*, In: Runco, Pritzker, 1999

Bonnefoy Y. (1975) Introduzione, in: Rimbaud, A., *Opere*, Mondadori, Milano

Borges J.L. (1975-81) *Tutte le opere*, Mondatori, Milano, 1985

Bosio A. C. (a cura di) (1979) *Sulla creatività*, Ed. Vita e Pensiero, Milano

Bowlby J. (1988) *Una base sicura*, Cortina, Milano

Bruner J. (1964) *Il conoscere. Saggi per la mano sinistra.* Armando, Roma, 1968

Bruner J. (1988) *La mente a più dimensioni.* Laterza, Roma-Bari

Bruner J., Jolly A., Sylva K. (a cura di) (1981) *Il gioco,* Armando, Roma, 1981

Buber M. (1925) *Il principio dialogico,* San Paolo, Cinisello Balsamo (MI), 1993

Caillois R. (1967) *I giochi e gli uomini. La maschera e la vertigine*, Bompiani, Milano, 1981

Campbell J. (1949) *L'eroe dai mille volti*, Feltrinelli, Milano, 1958

Canevaro A., Lippi G., Zanelli P. (1988) *Una scuola, uno sfondo*, Nicola Milano, Bologna

Carotenuto A. (1999) *Breve storia della psicoanalisi*, Bompiani, Milano

Carotenuto A. (1991) *Trattato di psicologia della personalità*, Cortina, Milano

Carriére J.C. (1998) *Il circolo dei contastorie*, Rizzoli, Milano

Cattanach A. (1999) *Process in the Arts Therapies*, Jessica Kingsley, London

Celan P., *Poesie*, a cura di G. Bevilacqua, Milano, Mondadori, 1998

Coleridge S.T. (1817) *Biografia literaria*, Editori Riuniti, Roma, 1991

Corbin H. (1958) *L'immaginazione creatrice. Le radici del sufismo*, Laterza, Bari, 2005

Corbin H. (1979) *Corpo spirituale e Terra celeste*, Adelphi, Milano, 1986

Courtney R. (1968) *Play, Drama & Thought*, Cassel, London

Courtney R. (1990) *Drama and Intelligence. A Cognitive Theory*, McGill-Queen's University Press, Montreal

Courtney R. (1995) *Drama and Feeling. An Aesthetic Theory*, McGill-Queen's University Press, Montreal

Csiszentmihalyi M. (1990) *Flow. The psychology of optimal experience*, Harper & Row, New York

Csiszentmihalyi M. (1996) *Creativity. Flow and the psychology of discovery and invention*, Harper & Row, New York

Currie G., Ravenscroft I. (2002) *Recreative Minds*, Clarendon Press, Oxford

Cytowic R.E. (1989) *Synesthesia: A Union of the Senses*, Springer Verlag, New York

Cytowic R.E. (1993) *The Man Who Tasted Shapes*, Putnam, New York

Dacey J., Lennon K. (1998) *Understanding Creativity*, Jossey-Bass, San Francisco (CA)

Damasio A.R. (1999) *Emozione e coscienza*, Adelphi, Milano, 2000

De Bono E. (1967) *Il pensiero laterale*, Rizzoli, Milano, 1969

De Bono E. (1970) *Creatività e pensiero laterale*, Rizzoli, Milano, 1998

Dewey J. (1934) *Art as Experience*, Perigee Books, New York, 2000

Dolci D. (1993) *Comunicare, legge della vita*, Lacaita, Manduria (BA)

Dostoevskij F. (1991) *Lettere sulla creatività*, Feltrinelli, Milano

Durand G. (1963) *Le strutture antropologiche dell'immaginario*, Dedalo, Bari, 1972

Durand G. (1999) *L'immaginazione simbolica*, RED, Como

Eakin P.J. (1999) *How Our Lives Become Stories: Making Selves*, Cornell University Press, Ithaca (NY)

Eaves M. (1982) *William Blake's Theory of Art*, Princeton University Press, Princeton (NJ)

Eisler R. (1987) *Il calice e la spada*, Frassinelli, Milano, 2006

Eliade M. (1964) *Il sacro e il profano*, Bollati Boringhieri, Torino, 1973

Eliot T.S. (1993) *Opere*, vol. I, II, trad di R. Sanesi, Bompiani, Milano

Erdoes R., Ortiz A. (a cura di) (1994) *Miti e leggende degli indiani d'America*, Mondadori, Milano

Ferraris M. (1996) *L'immaginazione*, Il Mulino, Bologna

Foster Damon S. (1988) *A Blake Dictionary*, University Press of New England, Hanover & London

Freud S. (1895) *Progetto di una psicologia*, in *Opere*, vol. II, Boringhieri, Torino, 1968

Freud S. (1912) *Consigli al medico nel trattamento psicoanalitico*, in *Opere*, vol. VI, Boringhieri, Torino, 1974

Freud S. (1915) *Metapsicologia*, in *Opere*, vol. VIII, Boringhieri, Torino, 1976

Fromm E. (1966) *Voi sarete come Dei*, Ubaldini, Roma, 1970

Galimberti U., (1992) *Dizionario di psicologia*, UTET, Torino

Garcia M.E.; Plevin M.; Macagno P. (2006) *Movimento creativo e danza*, Gremese, Roma

Gardner H. (1983) *Formae mentis. Saggio sulla pluralità dell'intelligenza*, Feltrinelli, Milano, 1987

Gardner H. (1993) *Creating Minds*, BasicBooks, New York

Garroni E. (1979) Voce: *Creatività*, in: Enciclopedia, Einaudi, Torino, 1979

Gazzaniga M.S., Ivry R.B. Manguin G.R. (2002) *Neuroscienze cognitive*, Bologna: Zanichelli, 2005

Gennaro A., Bucalo G. (2006) *La personalità creativa*, Laterza, Bari

Ghiselin B. (ed) (1952) *The Creative Process*, California University Press, Berkeley & Los Angeles

Givone S. (1978) *William Blake, Arte e Religione*, Mursia, Milano

Goffman E. (1974) *Frame Analysis*, Armando, Roma, 2001

Goleman D. (1995) *L'intelligenza emotiva*, Rizzoli, Milano, 1996

Goleman D., Ray M., Kaufman P. (1992) *Lo spirito creativo*, Rizzoli, Milano, 1999

Gombrich E.H. (1968) "Meditazioni su un cavalluccio, ovvero le radici della forma artistica", in: Whyte, 1968: 265-287

Goodman N. (1968) *I linguaggi dell'arte*, EST, Milano, 1998

Grainger R., Duggan M. (1997) *Imagination, Identification and Catharsis in Theatre and Therapy*, Jessica Kingsley, London

Grainger R. (1990) *Drama and Healing*, Jessica Kingsley, London

Grainger R. (1995) *The Glass of Heaven*, Jessica Kingsley, London

Grainger R. (1999) *Researching the Arts Therapies*, Jessica Kingsley, London

Grandin T. (1995) *Pensare in immagini*, Erickson, Trento, 2001

Graves R. (1955) *I miti greci*, Longanesi, Milano, 1983

Graves R.; Patai R. (1963) *I miti ebraici*, Longanesi, Milano, 1980

Greimas A.J. (1966) *Semantica strutturale*, Rizzoli, Milano, 1969

Hadamard J. (1945) *La psicologia dell'invenzione in campo matematico*, Milano: Cortina

Harris P.L. (2000) *The Work of the Imagination*, Blackwell, Oxford

Hillman J. (1972) *Il mito dell'analisi*, Adelphi, Milano, 1979

Huizinga J. (1939) *Homo ludens*, Einaudi, Torino, 1973

Jacobson R. (1963) *Saggi di linguistica generale*, Feltrinelli, Milano, 1966

Jennings S. (1998) *Introduction to Dramatherapy*, Jessica Kingsley, London

Jennings S., Minde, A. (1993) *Art Therapy and Dramatherapy. Masks of the Soul*, Jessica Kingsley, London

Johnstone K. (1979) *Impro*, Routledge, N.Y.

Johnstone K. (1999) *Impro for Storytellers*, Routledge, N.Y.

Jones P. (1996) *Drama as Therapy. Theatre as Living*, London/New York, Routledge

Jung C.G. (1942) *Paracelso come fenomeno spirituale*, in: *Opere*, vol. 13, Boringhieri, Torino, 1988

Jung C.G. (1912/1952) *Simboli della trasformazione*, in: *Opere*, vol. 5, Boringhieri, Torino, 1970

Jung C.G. (1921) *Tipi psicologici*, in : *Opere*, vol.6, Boringhieri, Torino, 1969

Jung C.G. (1928) *L'Io e l'inconscio*, in: *Opere*, vol. 7, Boringhieri, Torino, 1983

Jung C.G. (1950) "Prefazione alla traduzione inglese dell'I King", in: *Opere*, vol. 11, Boringhieri, Torino, 1979

Kabat-Zinn J. (2004) *Vivere momento per momento*, Corbaccio, Milano, 2005

Kast V. (1988) *Immaginazione attiva*, RED, Como, 1997

Kearney R. (1988) *The Wake of Imagination*, Routledge, London

Kelly G.A. (1963) *A Theory of Personality*, Norton, N.Y.

Kerényi K. (1963) *Gli dei e gli eroi della Grecia*, Mondatori, Milano, 1989

Koestler A. (1964), *The Act of Creation*, Macmillan, London

Köhler W. (1929) *La psicologia della Gestalt*, Feltrinelli, Milano, 1961

Kris E. (1952) *Ricerche psicoanalitiche sull'arte*, Einaudi, Torino, 1967

Kris E., Kurz, O. (1934) *La leggenda dell'artista*, Bollati Boringhieri, Torino, 1989

Lahad M. (2000) *Creative Supervision*, Jessica Kingsley, London

Landy R.J. (1995) The dramatic world view, in Jennings, ed. *Dramatherapy with Children and Adolescents*, Routledge, London, 1995

Landy R.J. (1993) *Persona and Performance*, Jessica Kingsley, London

Landy R.J. (2001) *New Essays in Drama Therapy*, C.C.Thomas, Springfield, IL.

Lanes S. (1980) *The Art of Maurice Sendak*, Harry N. Abrams, New York

Langer H. (1989) *Mindfulness*, Da Capo Press, Cambridge (MA)

Langer H. (1997) *The Power of Mindful Learning*, Da Capo Press, Cambridge (MA)

Leppmann W. (1981) *Rilke. La vita e l'opera*, Longanesi, Milano, 1989

Lévi-Strauss C. (1958) *Antropologia strutturale*, Il Saggiatore, Milano, 1966

Libet B., Gleason C. A., Wright E. W. and Pearl D. K. (1983) "Time of conscious intention to act in relation to onset of cerebral activity (readiness potential). The unconscious initiation of a freely voluntary act", *Brain*, 102, 623–642.

Libet B., Wright E. W. and Gleason C. A. (1982) "Readiness potentials preceding unrestricted spontaneous and preplanned voluntary acts", *Electroencephalography and Clinical Neurophysiology*, 54, 322–325.

Lubart T., Guignard J.-H. (2004) "The generality-specificity of creativity: a multivariate approach", in Sternberg et al., 2004

Lurija A. (1968) *Viaggio nella mente di un uomo che non dimenticava nulla*, Armando, Roma, 1979

Maduro R. (1976) *Artistic creativity in a Brahmin painter community*, Research monograph 14, Center for Southeast Asia Studies, University of California, Berkeley

Martindale C. (1999) "Biological Bases of Creativity", in Sternberg (ed), 1999, pp 137-152

Maslow A. (1954) *Motivazione e personalità*, Armando, Roma, 1973

Maslow A. (1962) *Verso una psicologia dell'essere*, Astrolabio, Roma, 1971

Mcniff S. (2004) *Art Heals. How creativity cures the soul*, Shambala, Boston & London

Mednick S.A. (1962) "The associative basis of the creative process", *Psychological Review*, 69, pp. 220-232

Meier C.A. (1985) *Il sogno come terapia*, Ed. Mediterranee, Roma, 1987

Melucci A. (a cura di) (1994) *Creatività: miti, discorsi, processi*, Feltrinelli, Milano

Menegazzo C. (1996) "Lavorare con l'immaginario per ritrovare la soglia dell'umano", *Psicodramma Analitico* n. 5, pp. 45-56

Merton R.K. (1968) *Teoria e struttura sociale*, Bologna: Il Mulino, 2000

Merton R.K., Barber, E.G. (2003) *Viaggi e avventure della Serendipity*, Il Mulino, Bologna

Montaigne M. de (1580-88) *L'immaginazione*, a cura di N. Panichi, Olschki, Perugia, 2000

Moon B. (ed.) (1997) *An Enciclopedia of Archetipal Symbolism*, Shambala, Boston & London

Moreno J.L. (1923) *Il teatro della spontaneità*. Guaraldi, Firenze, 1973

Moreno J.L. (1946) *Manuale di psicodramma*, vol. I, Astrolabio, Roma, 1985

Morin E. (1986) *La conoscenza della conoscenza*, Feltrinelli, Milano, 1989

Mottana P. (2002) *L'opera dello sguardo. Braci di pedagogia immaginale*, Moretti & Vitali, Bergamo

Movimento di Cooperazione Educativa (a cura di) (1978) "La creatività nell'espressione", *Quaderni di cooperazione educativa* n. 7, La Nuova Italia, 1978.

Nachmanovitch S. (1990) *Free Play. Improvisation in Life and Art*, Tarcher/Putnam, New York

Neisser U. (a cura di) (1993) *La percezione del sé*, Bollati Boringhieri, Torino, 1999

Obhi S.S., Haggard P. (2004) "Free Will and Free Won't" , *American Scientist*, July-August 2004, p. 358-365

Oliverio A. (2006) *Come nasce un'idea*, Rizzoli, Milano

Paley M. (1970) *Energy and the Imagination. A Study of the Development of Blake's Thought*, Oxford University Press, London

Perrault C. (1957) *I racconti di Mamma l'Oca*, Einaudi, Torino (ed.or. 1696)

Perussia F. (2000) *Storia del soggetto. La formazione mimetica della persona*, Bollati Boringhieri, Torino

Perussia F. (2003) *Theatrum Psychotechnicum. L'espressione poetica della persona*, Bollati Boringhieri, Torino

Pieri P.F. (1998) *Dizionario Junghiano*, Bollati Boringhieri, Torino

Pitruzzella, S. (2002) "States of grace. Transformative events in Dramatherapy", *Dramatherapy journal*, vol. 24, n. 2

Pitruzzella S. (2002a) "La funzione del pubblico nel teatro terapeutico", *Teatri della Diversità – Catarsi*, nn. 22-23

Pitruzzella S. (2003) *Persona e soglia. Fondamenti di Drammaterapia*, Armando, Roma

Pitruzzella S. (2004) *Manuale di Teatro Creativo*, Franco Angeli, Milano

Pitruzzella S. (2007) Introduzione, in : William Blake, *I Quattro Zoa*, Fondazione Piccolo di Calanovella, Capo D'Orlando, 2007

Platone, *Tutte le opere*, trad. di E. Martini, Sansoni, Firenze, 1993

Poincaré J.-H. (1908) *Scienza e metodo*, Torino: Einaudi, 1997

Radin P., Jung C. G., Kerényi K. (1954) *Il briccone divino*, Bompiani, Milano, 1965

Raine K. (1991) *Golgonooza. City of Imagination*, Lindisfarne Press, Hudson (NY)

Ramachandran V.S., Blakeslee S. (1998) *La donna che morì dal ridere*, Mondadori, Milano, 1999

Ribot T. (1900) *L'imagination créatrice*, Félix Alcan, Paris

Ricoeur P. (1976) *Imagination in discourse and in action*, in: Robinson, Rundell, 1994

Ricoeur P. (1990) *Sé come un altro*, Jaca Book, Milano, 1993

Ricoeur P. (1992) *La persona*, Morcelliana, Brescia, 1997

Riffard P. (1972) *L'esoterismo*, Rizzoli, Milano, 1976

Rilke R.M. (1903-8) *Lettere a un giovane poeta*, Adelphi, Milano, 1980

Rilke R.M., Salomé, L. (1975) *Epistolario*, La Tartaruga, Milano, 1984

Rizzolati G.; Sinigaglia C. (2006) *So quel che fai. Il cervello che agisce e i neuroni specchio*, Raffaello Cortina, Milano

Roberts R.M. (1989) *Serendipity. Accidental Discoveries in Science,* Wiley Science Edition, New York

Robinson G.; Rundell J. (1994) *Rethinking Imagination,* Routledge, London & New York

Rodari G. (1973) *Grammatica della fantasia,* Einaudi, Torino

Rodari G. (1981) *Esercizi di fantasia,* Editori Riuniti, Roma

Rodari G. (1983) *Il cane di Magonza,* Editori Riuniti. Roma

Rogers C.R. (1961) *La terapia centrata sul cliente,* Martinelli, Firenze, 1970

Roose-Evans J. (1989) *Experimental Theatre. From Stanislavskij to Peter Brook,* Routledge, London

Rothenberg A. (1979) *The Emerging Goddess,* The University of Chicago Press, Chicago

Rothenberg A. (1988) *The Creative Process of Psychotherapy,* Norton, New York

Rothenberg A. (1990) *Creativity and Madness,* The John Hopkins University Press, Baltimore

Rothenberg A., Hausman C.R. (eds.) (1976) *The Creativity Question,* Duke University Press, Durham (NC)

Runco M. (2004) "Everyone has creative potential", in Sternberg, R.J. et al. (eds.), 2004

Runco M., Pritzker, S. (1999) *Enciclopedia of Creativity,* Academic Press, San Diego (CA)/London

Sawyer R.K. (2006) *Explaining Creativity: The Science of Human Innovation,* Oxford University Press, New York

Scabia G. (1976) *Marco Cavallo: un'esperienza di animazione in un ospedale psichiatrico,* Einaudi, Torino

Slade P. (1954) *Child Drama,* University of London Press Ltd, London

Slade P. (1968) *Experience of Spontaneity,* Longman, London

Slade P. (1995) *Child Play. Its importance for human development,* Jessica Kingsley, London

Sontag F. (1988) *Truth and Imagination,* University Press of America, Lanham (MA)

Sparti D. (2005) *Suoni inauditi,* Il Mulino, Bologna

Sperry R. (1981) "Some Effects of Disconnecting the Cerebral Hemispheres", Nobel Lecture, http://nobelprize.org

Spolin V. (1963) *Improvisation for the Theater,* Northwestern University Press, Evanston, IL

Stein E. (1917) *L'empatia.* A cura di M. Nicoletti, Franco Angeli, Milano, 1985

Stern D.N. (1985) *Il mondo interpersonale del bambino,* Bollati Boringhieri, Torino, 1987

Sternberg R.J. (ed.) (1999) *Handbook of Creativity,* Cambridge University Press, Cambridge

Sternberg R.J. et al. (eds.) (2004) *Creativity. From Potential to Realization,* American Psychological Association, Washington, DC

Tillich P. (1952) *Il coraggio di esistere,* Astrolabio, Roma, 1968

Tirinnanzi N. (1997) *Umbra naturae. L'immaginazione in Bruno e Ficino,* Edizioni di storia e letteratura, Roma

Toms M. (ed.) (1997) *The Well of Creativity,* Hay House Inc., Carlsbad, CA

Torrance E.P. (1995) *Why Fly? A Philosophy of Creativity,* Ablex Publishing Corporation, Norwood (NJ)

Trombetta C. (1989) *La Creatività. Un'utopia contemporanea,* Bompiani, Milano

Tselikas-Portmann E. (1999) *Supervision and Dramatherapy,* Jessica Kingsley, London

Valeri V. (1979) "Gioco", in: *Enciclopedia,* Einaudi, Torino

Van Gennep A. (1909) *I riti di passaggio,* Boringhieri, Torino, 1981

Vegetti Finzi S. (1986) *Storia della psicoanalisi,* Mondatori, Milano

Vygotskij L.S. (1930) *Immaginazione e creatività nell'età infantile,* Edititori Riuniti, Roma, 1972

Wallas G. (1926) *The Art of Thought,* Hartcourt Brace, London

Weston J. (1920) *Indagine sul Santo Graal,* Sellerio, Palermo, 1992

Whyte L.L. (1960) *L'inconscio prima di Freud,* Astrolabio, Roma, 1970

Whyte L.L. (1968), *Aspetti della forma,* Dedalo, Bari, 1977

Wilshire B. (1982) *Role-Playing and Identity. The Limits of Theatre as Metaphor,* Indiana University Press, Bloomington

Winnicott D.W. (1971) *Gioco e realtà,* Armando, Roma, 1979

Yates F. (1964) *Giordano Bruno e la tradizione ermetica,* Laterza, Bari, 1989

Yates F. (1966) *L'arte della memoria,* Boringhieri, Torino, 1972

Printed in the United States
by Baker & Taylor Publisher Services